Vulnerability is courage in you, weakness in me

TAP

INTO

GREATNESS

[
**HOW TO STOP MANAGING
START LEADING
AND DRIVE BIGGER IMPACT**
]

LET'S GO!

SARAH SINGER-NOURIE

Ripple Press, LLC
2248 Meridian Blvd. Suite H Minden, NV 89423
Printed in theUnited States of America
First Edition: April 2015

ISBN: 978-0-9776518-3-2

Table of Contents:

Chapter 0: Let's Go! . . . . Page 11

Chapter 1: The Third Who . . . . Page 19

Chapter 2: WIIFM . . . . Page 27

Chapter 3: Your Process . . . . Page 35

Chapter 4: Your Options . . . . Page 49

Chapter 5: Impact Is ALL You . . . . Page 57

Chapter 6: Setting Yourself Up . . . . Page 67

Chapter 7: Coaching Them To Impact . . . . Page 79

Chapter 8: Playing Bigger . . . . Page 91

Chapter 9: State . . . . Page 105

Chapter 10: VAK . . . . Page 121

Chapter 11: More Power Than You Know . . . . Page 139

Chapter 12: The Three Ingredients . . . . Page 153

Chapter 13: Pyramid of Perspective . . . . Page 167

Chapter 14: Making It Stick . . . . Page 177

Chapter 15: Above the Line . . . . Page 191

Chapter 16: The Beginning . . . . Page 203

Chapter Resources . . . . Page 209

Acknowledgements . . . . Page 216

A Bit About Me . . . . Page 218

For Colin, who fuels me

And my parents, whose belief in me caused huge ripples.

True Source:

Every concept in this book grew out of what I've experienced, applied, dismantled or evolved from what I've learned from other people.

I was lucky to be thrown into the world of personal development for my own life-altering experience in a program called SuperCamp[1] at age 15. At 16, I was teaching teachers in my school how they could do it better, at 16 being coached by maters on how to facilitate transformative experiences for others, at 22, teaching others how to teach and facilitate, and by 28 co-authored my first book on it. I was jokingly referred to as the poster kid for this work as it seemed that I grew up in it. I've been teaching the concepts in this book in some form for over twenty years.

While I'm creating new distinctions and tools all the time, much of what I teach, captured in this book, is work that's become part of who I am over decades of teaching and coaching it. Some of these concepts have been in the self-development world for years and I'm giving them new distinctions and application to your world as a leader here. Some are evolutions of concepts I co-created or learned with other master coaches.

While I've noted sources and experts for many concepts throughout the book, the following masters have had such indelible impact in my development and thinking that I still hear their voices in my head and my work every day, years later. Their influence is woven throughout this book, and if you don't have their work on your shelf and in your practice, seek it out. They include (in alphabetical order, since they're impossible to rank):

Linda Brown
Bobbi Deporter
Eric Jensen
Mark Reardon
Blair Singer
Maggie Weiss

To every one of you, thank you for your ruthless support, coaching, impact, collaboration and most of all- your shared commitment to what's possible in the world.

Power whoosh of love and immeasurable gratitude,
Sarah

Moving the Dial
by Blair Singer

The eternal quest in sports, in business and in life has always been the same—"how to get better." How to eke out that extra dollar, extra productivity, extra edge.

I remember long, scorching runs up and down the hills and country roads of northeastern Ohio in the 1960s as our small cross-country team ran mile after mile, each of us looking for a few more seconds to ultimately shave off our times. We pushed, we sweated, we drove, we were up before daylight and still running as the sun slipped from view at the end of the day.

It was in those times that I learned the meaning of searching for that extra gear inside. All these years later, I have worked with thousands of organizations and hundreds of thousands of individuals, helping them increase sales and build championship teams—all on the same quest. The goal is always the same: to ultimately "move the dial" or make a noticeable change in results.

Certainly pushing harder, becoming more skilled, more disciplined and invoking tighter accountability would seem to drive better results. But what if there was another way?

Nearly every person I have ever met believes there is a bigger, better person inside of them. Whether they find it or not is another issue, but they all believe it to be true. The question is—how do you get to it? What if there was a way to move the dial without having to set outrageous goals, create magical incentives, employ charismatic leaders or search for the perfect dream team?

I have worked with enough people to observe that inside each person is a piece of magic, a passion, a desire to tap their own brilliance for no other reason than to fulfill their human desire to find that greatness inside themselves.

Yet most will continue to wallow in mediocrity, cynicism and excuses for most of their lives and careers unless something comes along to light them up.

Sarah understands this situation intimately. As a teenager, anyone could see Sarah had "potential" but was sliding quickly in the wrong direction. Something had to change. The school system was not helping her, her friends were not helping her and she needed help. She was in trouble, with failing grades and compromised spirit. Through the support of a few great mentors, Sarah found herself in a teen development program during the summer of her sophomore year of high school. Something hit! Something unlocked! Something turned her around to the degree that when she returned from that program, she was on fire. She had learned how to learn and how to find that gear of brilliance inside. SO much so that she started teaching her teachers how to find that magic in their students. She got a degree in education, became a worldwide expert in the use of alternative and accelerated learning methodologies and has gone on to transform the lives of thousands of individuals and scores of organizations.

Having been in the business of training for over 25 years, I can tell you we have passed a pivotal point in the world of human development in business. It used to be that a company could give its teams basic business and technical skills and could expect a lift in their productivity. Yet the complexity of the world we live in has created an accelerating blizzard of choices, challenges, obstacles, temptations and distractions that can de-rail the best-laid plans.

Once an option, it is now imperative that any organization or individual hoping to survive and flourish must obtain personal development skills to successfully navigate that world. And while many companies give lip service to the idea, it is only visionary leaders who understand and have the courage to open the door to the world of emotion, passion and spirit.

It is these leaders who are now blazing new trails into the realm of unprecedented results, magical creativity and amazing income. By understanding how we learn and how to manage the mental and emotional quotients, you can begin to reach inside yourself and everyone on your team to help them find that magical gear that catapults them to extraordinary results.

Moving the dial is more than managing numbers, more than managing plans and strategies. Today and going forward, it is about truly Tapping the Greatness that has been waiting to be ignited inside us all. I know you are in good hands as you read this book. I know Sarah's story well, because she is my sister. If you ever meet her, you will know that the spirit of possibility, brilliance and life exudes from her like a starburst. To be a great leader of people, you must believe there is greatness inside you and in those around you. This book is your primer to tapping that greatness.

Be awesome.

- Blair Singer,
Entrepreneur, best-selling author of *SalesDogs, Team Code of Honor, Little Voice Mastery*, Rich Dad Advisor

"You're going to be the one..."

Chapter 0: Let's Go!

Of all the questions a person can ask, two have defined most of my life: *Why?* and *What if?*

They've inspired me to take things apart to figure out how they could work. And put them back together, better.

"Why does that happen?" followed by "I'll figure it out" ...until I did.

"What if it XXX were possible?" followed by "I'll mess with it to figure out how to make it possible" ...until I could.

As a kid I drove adults crazy with those incessant questions. They caused me to hear every 'no' from someone as a challenge to find a different angle which would get me a yes. *"Hmm... why not? I'll find a different way to ask the question."*

While these questions got me into trouble in school, from elementary school through my graduate degree as I disrupted the system, they're also the very questions which have instigated positive change for every initiative I've ever touched, and brought this book into your hands. More on that if you'd like in the *A Bit About Me* chapter, but for now, know that questions like these have fueled and been answered by this book:

- Why can you sometimes crush it and other times flop with the exact same approach?
- Why were we never taught how to really influence or lead?
- Why do four leaders try the same strategy and get four wildly different results?
- Why can't I get through to XYZ person?
- What if we could decode the secrets to influence and inspiration?
- What if you could be consistently awesome as a leader instead

of sporadically great?
- What if you knew how to motivate anyone?
- What if you could authentically choose and change your mood on demand?

If any of those questions intrigue you, you're in the right place. So let's get the specifics clear.

Who?
You! This book is meant for you if you're in a position of influence with others, and suspect you could be having more consistently awesome impact than you are now. The tools here are currently used with powerful effect by the thousands of executives, entrepreneurs, managers, team leaders, trainers, parents, educators and coaches across several industries, professional, educational and athletic worlds I've coached in the last few decades.

So while you may have a title of "leader" right now, this is about going beyond your title to become the person they remember ten years after they've worked with you, as the one who made permanently positive impact on how they think, the way they make things happen, and how they define their own horizon. You'll be the person who not only led them in their work, but unlocked possibility for them as people.[1]

The Other Who?
Me. I consult, teach and coach individuals, groups and companies large and small to transform individuals into impactful influencers and groups into high performing teams. I get called in by leaders to coach them to their next level of clarity and strategic impact, help startups launch with intentional culture in place, guide organizations through disruptive change, take high-potentials to superstar performer level, and jumpstart learning or teaching where it normally flatlines. You can get my backstory on page 218.

What?
Every piece of this book is about how to unlock and expand the deep well of talent, insight and possibility within people beyond the capacity

you've seen. Those people include every person you touch in your path as a leader every day, and you, too.Designed for you to learn quickly, apply immediately and get results from consistently, you're holding the best core set of frameworks, tools and strategies to bring out inspired potential and performance in others and yourself. This is not another "you should" book of ideas without practical application- it's the opposite. I've worked the kinks out of the theory through practical application for you over years of leading teams and coaching across industries in the corporate, nonprofit, entrepreneurial and educational worlds, and have distilled it into a book for you here. Behind it, I continuously analyze leaders of all kinds (from horrible to brilliant), learn from the best gurus[2] out there in personal development, study the findings of neuroscience applied to learning and performance and closely watch the nuanced impact people have on one another in a way others miss. I've experimented in thousands of scenarios, challenges and teams. From it all, I've re-engineered the best practices, deciphered the Whys behind their repeatable effect, re-contextualized concepts you may have missed before and created simple paths to layered impact... into an approach you can learn and repeat. The approach you're about to learn has become the way great leaders lead at a greater level of impact than anyone just focused on managing ever could.

Where and When?

Well, you're holding this book and are ultimately in control of how this goes, but know that it's definitely a process- something that you will both work on deliberately and will work itself through for you in the background of what you do every day. Becoming the kind of leader who impacts people the way I'm proposing has multiple parts to it, so give yourself some space to connect them all. While there will be definite "Oh yeah- let's GO!" moments for you in this book of getting a concept, trying it out right away, and noticing a difference in the response you get, others will take more marination time in your mind. Some ideas in here are uncomplicated, yet deeply layered; they might seem obvious at first, yet when you get into them you'll realize they require some re-racking of your thinking or retraining of your responses. Some won't connect until later, maybe when you least expect it. That's how real-life learning happens most potently. I suggest reading the book cover-to-cover the first time and then go back in whatever order makes sense for you to really try the concepts out. You could easily take them on one at a time in order (they build on one another) or you could try them depending on what applies in the moment for you. I love *just in time learning*, which is bringing the right tool in at exactly the moment it's truly needed in real life- so it solves or answers something for you in real time and sticks long-term as practical learning rather than just a theoretical concept to try someday. Ultimately, each chapter will become its own reference point for you, and you'll come back to them again and again to brush up or zoom in on a particular tool for deeper or more focused application in your world. I've got many layers of support for you[3] to take these concepts further into your practice, but let's start with this book.

How?

I know that you've been to training sessions and read listicles and books that offer things like the '21 tips to becoming a better manager' or '9 steps to XYZ.' I've heard and seen all that too. This is not a series of steps to walk through, but rather a dynamic process which will be interactive. Throughout it, I'll be creating images and scenes for you. I will give you some scripts to run in your head and even out loud in particular scenarios. I might press some internal buttons which bring up some emotions for you. I'll definitely challenge you to try some things- like physical movements[4] which will cement concepts into your memory more easily or tactics to go try out with real people in your world. Everyone likes to think they are unique and have a fresh approach, but I promise you, you'll be be stretching yourself in some new ways here. I'm always surprised by how different this approach feels for folks compared to what they're seen/heard/experienced be- fore.

The 'how' is pretty important in this case. I won't make you any promises. I can't, because tapping your own greatness as a leader is a shift you'll own yourself. I *will* absolutely show you how, and give you the perspective and tools I've honed into a straightforward approach that's quickly impactful as you apply it. My biggest concern is always more in the what-you-do-with-it part than the theory part, but you'll get both here. If you don't see how you can apply these ideas or are getting the results you want as you apply your learning from this book, send me an email and we'll work through it together. Meanwhile, I'm going to bring some new layers to the way you think, new approaches to the way you assess and create impact. You'll understand what happened, why it happened and how to either repeat its impact yourself or keep it from happening again. I'll also give you some pretty straightforward "try this" tools for situations you're facing now, which can be solved or inspired much faster than you'd guess. I'm a fan of more with less... why not try a single approach with which you can solve the issue without drama AND instill confidence in someone AND teach them something that will stick permanently AND energize everyone involved all at once? You can. These tools are layered in that way for multiple outcomes, steeped in brain science, personal development and accelerated learning, all of which became my passions at a very young age- and I have been fortunate enough to devote my life to. But only because I knew early on the way most people do things just wasn't for me.

Which brings us to the most important question...

Why?

Because there's another way. A better way.
This is not a management book, because I believe you can do way better than that. Managing implies a base level of holding it all together without things falling apart.
"He's having trouble managing his temper."
"That's a lot to carry- do you think you can manage it all?"
"I've just got to manage my time and it'll all get done."
"Who's managing this project?"
None of those are very inspired. Managing means it's continuing to operate or run without disaster. I would hope so. Got it, and so do you. From here forward, I'm going to assume that you can already manage- keep things running by whatever means you need to. So on these pages we're going to elevate the conversation and go way beyond that- to grow how you influence, create, inspire, impact and shape both what

happens and the people in your world... how you lead.
Because you can.

I'm here to tell, show and teach you how you can have the kind of impact that unleashes awesomeness in the people around you every day... and that what it takes to do so isn't rocket science. You've got a brilliant leader inside you, actually have the ability (whether you know it or not) to consistently inspire and tap the brilliant thinkers, performers, creators and team members inside those unsuspecting folks around you right now.

I know that if you're still reading this far into it, you've got the inclination to have impact, so that's huge. Because, while I'll provide the tools and process, ultimately the impact is all on you. You're going to be the one to open up your people's possibility, to truly tap their greatness. Are you ready?

Let's go!

Notes:

"Either direction it steers you, it's an important force of influence in everything you do. So pay attention to it."

Chapter 1:
The Third Who
(and the glue for the rest of this book)

Before we move forward, let's clarify who's in this conversation with us.

There are a few:

1. YOU... definitely the most important person in this book. While we will talk all about how to tap into everyone else's greatness, really this is about YOU, the one doing that tapping every day (or not), every minute you're not here reading.

2. Me... of course I'm here as your guide on the side, challenger of your patterns, mirror-holder for what you may not be seeing about yourself and coach who believes in the leader you have yet to reveal.

3. But then there's a third WHO in this conversation...

That little voice inside your head

What little voice? That one—the one that just said, "What's she talking about? I don't have a little voice inside my head." Yeah, that's the one. You've got one. We've all got one, and that's a good thing, especially if we're aware of it. That voice is what keeps you from jumping into oncoming traffic, putting your hand on a hot stove or going down a creepy alley after dark. It's constantly assessing what's happening in your world against what it thinks is a good idea for you. So it pipes up in favor of, in opposition to, or distracting you away from whatever's going on in front of you. It has a running commentary and strong opinions about what you're doing and how you're doing it. It can inspire you, protect you or psyche you out. It can also bug you about a particular thing until something shifts and you do something about it.

Your little voice is the third Who, right here in the mix as you read these words, with us.

It's also what we have in common, and is foundational for everything else I'll teach you in this book. You, the people you'd like to influence (especially the challenging ones), and I may have one critically important refrain coming from our little voice. The thing that has *powered me*[1] through all the conflict I created and all the difference I've made in the way people teach and lead, is a persistent complaint that might be familiar to you and to the people you'd like to influence right now. It may also drive what your team is thinking about their same-old routine, or why you picked up this book as a leader...

"There's got to be a better way."

Have you ever had that thought as you were cringing through another conflict with the same person again? Sitting through another incredibly boring meeting or conference call? Watching your audience glaze over during a presentation? Of course you have. And so has your team.

Where this becomes an edge for me and benefit for you here is that I don't ever just let it go. "There's got to be a better way" pairs with "What if...." and gnaws at me until I do something about it. I experiment, strategize, research and re-experiment until I solve it with a better way. Like how to truly lead with impact, (hence this book). I'll keep solving because refinement is continuous. I've taught every concept in this book at least 500 times, and every time I do I get a new facet of it, a better refinement of it.

So that's a great example of that little voice acting as a catalyst for something awesome, as it often is. It can cause inspiration or get you to your best. Except when it doesn't, which is also the case sometimes. It can cause mischief in your thinking, or psyche you out.

Truthfully, many of us have competing voices a lot of the time. Think cheerleader on one shoulder, critic on the other—a more accurate depiction of what's really going on in there than the angel-devil image we've seen in movies.

Dr. Martin Seligman, known as the originator of "positive psychology" coined the phrase "learned helplessness" and is the foremost researcher on our internal dialogue's impact. Patterns in how that little voice talks to us *optimistically or pessimistically* determine our resilience, and how quickly we give up or stick with something when it doesn't go well. Seligman explains that much of it comes down to the "explanatory style" of our little voice- how we explain negative and positive events to ourselves. Your *explanatory style*[2] has three important parts, Permanence, Pervasiveness, and Personalization:

How you explain...	Pessimistic	Optimistic
Permanence how permanent an event *seems* to me	**Bad events seem *permanent*-explained in *always* or *never*:** "This is never going to work." "I'm not a math person." "He's always on me." "This failure was about stupidity." **Positive events seem *temporary*:** "I had a good day." "I got lucky in guessing the right questions to prepare for." • May give up even after success, believing it was a fluke. • Helplessness kicks in quicker.	**Bad events seem *temporary*, from temporary causes:** "I'm too frustrated right now to do this." "It'll go very differently after we rerack." **Positive events seem permanent, from fixed causes, traits, abilities:** "This is my sweet spot- I'm great at this." "They've got nothing on us." • Try harder after success, believing that they'll succeed again. • Resilience is a clear pattern.
Pervasive how contained an event is in my life	**Bad events are *universal*:** "It's no use." "Relationships suck." Catastrophize events- one bad thing happens, and it all falls apart. **Positive events are caused by *specific* factors:** "I crushed that presentation just now." "This idea is working because it's just the two of us trying it."	**Bad events are *specific*:** "It didn't work because we didn't get this one big piece right." "This relationship isn't working for me." **Positive events are *universal*:** "I'm awesome. " "This is a great idea."
Personal who I blame for how things go	**We blame ourselves when bad things happen (Internalize):** "I suck." "I'm just not a math person." "I completely bombed." **We attribute good things happening to factors outside of ourself (Externalize):** "The team created a great presentation for me to deliver." "They were relaxed, so it went well."	**We blame circumstances or other people when bad things happen (Externalize):** "You suck." "I have had some serious challenges with math." "It was a horrible setup from the beginning." **We believe that we cause good things to happen (Internalize):** "I won over every skeptic in that room." "I was relaxed going into it, so everyone else relaxed too."

Whatever direction it steers you, your little voice is an important force of influence in everything you do. *So pay attention to it.*

The other voices

Just like you, every person you're with or trying to influence at any moment also has the little voice/s yammering away at them. So while you might be the one up in front or with the title, speaking at any given time, there are a lot of other inaudible voices in the room competing with you. An accurate roll call in your last meeting would include your actual voice, which has the floor, and your internal little voice, and all the little voices inside every head of the people 'listening' (or not) to you in the conversation, possibly all silently speaking at once while you're the only one audible in the room. And you thought you really had the floor? Maybe.

At any given time, the voice in someone's head as you're talking/interacting with them is doing one of the following:
1. It's agreeing and connecting with you, all in, ready to go with you.
2. It's questioning, resisting or disagreeing with you.
3. It needs to be heard so you can get another point of view or it needs to be won over. It's distracted and not even listening, and needs to be refocused to get back into the game.

You want their voice with you, in position #1, yes? Ultimately. But before you start trying to win them over, know that if their voice is questioning you, it could be because there's a genius idea (different from yours) brewing in there. Or there could be some decent feedback for you about why they're not in agreement. If you can just get inside their heads, right?

Here's how to start:

1. Start noticing your own little voice and where it's pointing

For the next few conversations/hours/days, observe what's going on in your own head while you interact with others and go about otherwise normal activity. Where does your little voice pipe up? When you're doing great? When you're flailing? When someone else is talking? Awareness and exposure to it starts to give you some options of what to do with it and how to channel it.

• *Notice patterns.*
  Are there certain situations that trigger your inner critic every time? Cut them off at the pass. Situations in which your voice keeps pestering you about the same issue? Maybe it's time to address the

issue. Conditions that summon a certain voice? Maybe it's best to not make decisions when you're really upset, as the voice isn't rational, and you regret it later every time.

- ***Get mastery.***
The truth is that this topic is huge, and takes more than a few tips to truly master. It's worth doing, as it truly pilots everything you do. The single best source on this topic for you is Blair Singer—start with his *Little Voice Mastery* book and system.

2. Consider their little voices

As you start to notice your own little voice a bit more, consider that everyone you interact with has their own little voice, too. Imagine what their voice might be saying, and pay attention to cues you can see from the outside (facial expression, eye movements, body language, pauses).

3. Address the voice/s in the room.

If you know that their little voice is working in the background of your conversation in a particular way (like doubting or criticizing), call it out. "You may be doubting whether or not we can do this, based on how it went last time. That's understandable. Here's what's completely different now..."

Calling out what's been silently working against you de-powers it, like turning on bright lights in a dark, creepy room. It's all still there, but now you can see what you're dealing with clearly and directly.

In a group, calling out voices like this is liberating for everyone involved—often you can hear an audible sigh of relief as everyone relaxes a little.

A particular voice to look out for:
The Skeptic

If you know yourself as a skeptic or would like to influence one, know that this is an important foe to be aware of as a leader, and is simply a product of a loud little voice.

I believe that a skeptic is really just an optimist who's been hardened

over time by too many layers of disappointment in what they thought was possible, so they've steeled themselves against more disappointment by disengaging or convincing themselves with a mantra of "it's not possible." Usually they have competing little voices at work in their heads—one that's still under there, asking, "What if I/we could...?" and a louder one drowning it out with "It's NOT possible, let me remind you of all the times we've failed with that naive thinking." I love working with skeptics and resistant learners because I get them. We've got the same core vision. They've just allowed theirs to get buried
under a bunch of defensive negativity and I didn't.

Here's the key to the skeptic voice, should yours pop up during this process (likely) or you encounter one in your path:

- ***First acknowledge the doubt as real.***
  Acknowledging it doesn't mean you're agreeing with it. You're just identifying it as real for them (but not the only option). If you skip this step, then you come off as a pollyanna—either just pretending or actually believing that everything's all rainbows and unicorns, refusing to see the possible reality of why things don't work. That's the quickest way to get a skeptic to dismiss you completely, so call it out.

- ***Tap the core.***
  Once you demonstrate your understanding of their concerns, they're listening. Next, quickly move on to finding their pliable center of optimism—way beneath that exterior crust of negativity. You can get there by addressing, mapping and showing them possibility, and watching how they respond. When you touch on parts they care about, you'll see signs[3]. More on how to accurately show them the right possibility in the next chapter.

- ***Prove it.***
  As you take steps toward what's possible, keep calling it out. Their voice will want to dismiss forward steps as lucky or some other fluke. Fortunately, you'll be there as the coach on the sidelines to confirm, "There it is! This can be done! We're on our way."

Notes:

"It's the question in everyone's head, all the time..."

Chapter 2: WIIFM
The Ever-present Guide

What if you could actually get people hooked and psyched with your idea, your request, your viewpoint every time? Even that skeptic?

Completely possible.

We've already established that everyone's got that little voice in our heads. So let's get a handle on how to get those voices on your side, and keep them engaged. For the folks you'd like to influence, their internal voices could be speaking much louder inside their heads than you are on the outside. Sorry, it's not personal. That voice has the advantage of residency in there a lot longer than you have. Fortunately, there's a shortcut to get the little voice/s all in, ready to go with you.

Influence

That voice questions authority, and cautions us before we do something. It's also the determining voice that tells us to make the next move, or don't. Thousands of times every day, we're making decisions forward from one thing to the next, one step at a time, so quickly that we don't even notice all of them. Most of the time that voice is quietly piloting us in our seamless movement throughout the day, but sometimes it gets challenged, and pauses us. It pipes up in our head and asks the question: "Why should I do this?"

Put another way, it considers a next move or a request/directive from outside (i.e., another person) and goes right to the heart of it: "What's In It For Me?"

Bingo. WIIFM. That's the big question, and hugely important before your next interaction with someone. Why?

WIIFM is the question in everyone's head, all the time.

It's not always in an entitled you-need-to-give-me something voice (but sometimes it is). More often it's in an I-need-a-compelling-reason voice. Reason to change position, to do something different from what I already planned, to listen to what you have to say. Those thousands of micro-decisions we make all day come from this question too—there's something in it for us to make the next move, so we make it. Not everyone's WIIFM question is as brash or loud as mine was/is, but make no mistake—it's always there behind that squint in their eye.

In fact, it was likely there for you as you started this book..."Okay, what am I going to get out of this? What's in it for me to go through this whole book and do the things that Sarah challenges me to do?"
If you don't have those answers yet, you probably skipped the Intro chapter, so just pop back to page 1. If that doesn't do it, email or call me. Yes, I'm serious.

Going forward, the bigger question is: How are you utilizing the little voice or answering the WIIFM in other people's heads as you approach and lead them?

Because we know from our own experience that the voice in their heads has more leverage than you do on the outside, WIIFM has to get answered or you're wasting your breath. You can use it to your advantage to make communication smoother, points stickier (as in sticks in their heads longer), agreement happen faster, and learning more engaging (like they get it the first time, so no need for several more asks).

Answer the WIIFM, and you're in.
For many leaders, this is one of the hardest concepts to get their heads around, but ultimately one of the biggest game-changers. Often at this point I hear the following: "What's in it for them is to get to keep doing their job." or "But I don't really care what's in it for them—that's their issue. It's their job to do what I said, and I shouldn't have to sell them on it."

Yes, if they work for you, it is their job to technically do what you say. And yet, human motivation is a lot more complex than that. If you don't give them a WIIFM, it doesn't mean they *won't* do what you say. It just might take a lot longer to get done, the quality of what they produce won't be as great, you might need to re-explain it before they start it, and their buy-in to everything else might drop (which is contagious- reference Chapter #9: State).

Think about your own results as the best example. Recall a time when you produced something you were personally fired up about or invested in. Now recall a time when you produced or completed something simply because you had to, were supposed to, or were told to. Pretty different results in quality or time/process it took, and your personal experience to get there, right?

In Daniel Pink's awesome book *Drive*[1], he reminds us of the three biggest elements of human motivation:
1. Autonomy: it's MY choice, not someone else's
2. Mastery: I get to see my own progress, and it's achievable
3. Purpose: I get to be part of something bigger than myself.
   If you hit one of these, you've tapped WIIFM.

The other fair reason to address WIIFM at the onset is that even if they are invested in what you're about to ask/present, their thinking might be somewhere else at the time, such as the last meeting they came from, the last thing they were just working on before you approached, the last tweet they just posted, a particularly significant moment from some other part of their world that's working itself out in their head. How many times have you found yourself thirty seconds into a conversation before realizing that you haven't engaged yet or didn't really hear anything that person said because you haven't transitioned yet and the other person didn't really engage you effectively yet? There you go. Giving them a WIIFM gets them focused and present and engaged with you in the conversation.

Either way, just know that without the WIIFM you're assuming a whole lot about whether or not they're really with you for the rest of the conversation. And honestly, your time and energy is too valuable to waste repeating yourself unnecessarily because they didn't get it or weren't with you the first time.

So, address the persistent question of WIIFM first and get them hooked into the conversation. Then you are golden.

Here's how...

1. Get out of your own head for a minute.
Reflect and put yourself in their shoes for a moment.
Some key questions can help you get there...

What do they care about?
Some good guesses you can try out:
• Being the expert
• Being part of something significant
• Being part of a team
• Being the one who solved it or made it happen

What do they really want out of what they do?
Usually, it's as simple as:
• The opportunity to create or contribute something
• Acknowledgment
• Accomplishment

Why do they ultimately do what they do?
This is a deeper level, which we'll explore later in Chapter #13: Pyramid Of Perspective, but if you already know this answer for someone, here's where you employ it practically, tapping their Big Why with what you're presenting/asking.

Calling out what's been silently working against you de-powers it, like turning on bright lights in a dark, creepy room. It's still there, but now you can see what you're dealing with clearly. In a group, calling out voices like this is liberating for everyone involved—often you can hear an audible sigh of relief as everyone relaxes a little.

2. Make your ask/case/request from their perspective, answering one of the questions in #1 in it.

Seriously, in that request or directive that you just gave them, what was in it for them? What's really juicy for them in the agenda you're about to present? What opportunity is really there for them in the new project that you're considering? Compelling people open with your WIIFM, and have you hooked from the beginning. They speak to your needs first.

Some tools to open with their WIIFM:
- Think about what you know bugs them the most and make this the solution to it.
- Consider what their role or contribution in it can really cause, make easier, or solve.
- Open with the part they care about most.
- Start with them and their important part in the whole, not the whole first with them as a detail in it or a "therefore you need to..." at the end.

3. Start with a question you know will get a "Yes" or an "I'm in."

I did it with you at the beginning of this chapter, and you chose to read on. Decent online writers do it in the first line of a post so you click further. I teach teachers to do it at the beginning of everything they teach, and their students engage in learning immediately.

Try:
- *What if you could...*
  (fill in with something from the list above—what they care about, what they might want) "What if you could be the one who brought sense and structure to this whole thing that the team's been challenged with?"
- *Would you be interested in...*
  (fill in with something you know they'd like to be a part of) "Would you be interested in being a part of something that will make all the difference in the way this project goes?" or "Would you be

interested in some feedback that could take your presentation to a whole other level of awesome?"

• *Have you ever...*
(plural=How many of you...) "Have you ever wished we could have a way to approach these projects that could save us time, hassle and redundant meetings?"

Tip: I always have a series of three HMOY (how many of you) questions ready, so I'm ensured of a "Yes" or some kind of engagement from everyone in the room.
The first is serious: "HMOY would like to conquer the little voice?"
The second is funny, loosening up those who didn't raise their hands the first time: "HMOY would like to conquer someone else's little voice?"
The third is absurd, delivered with a chuckle, and the group holdouts finally engage because they get that I'm not going away: "HMOY can hear my voice right now?"

As you mess with this approach, remember that everyone's WIIFM is there all the time, most people are easier than you think to engage most of the time, and very few people's WIIFM get direct answers very often. It's a distinction that separates truly great leaders we want to follow from managers who leave us uninspired. The truly great leaders help us understand what's in it for us to follow them. They recognize the value of our work, our efforts, our time and our attention, and give us a reason to jump in from the beginning. They help us understand the outcomes and how those are connected to our own greatness. So now, that leader will be you.

Go try it!

Notes:

To Inspire others to love what they do
& trickle the inspiration down

"...it changes the game completely for them, and feels like slamming on the brakes when they were in cruise mode."

Chapter 3:
Your Process
(and theirs, too, so let's get this)

Have you...

- Ever gotten into an argument with someone and couldn't think of your best comebacks until hours later?
- Ever been impatient the last time someone just wasn't getting it as fast as you needed them to?
- Ever wondered how a great athlete like Wayne Gretzky could be such a massive failure as a coach?
- Noticed yourself thinking about WIIFM now—sort of newly awkward self-awareness trying it or "Doh!"moments of hindsight realizing where you could've addressed it?

Could these four scenarios be related? Absolutely.

Every one of them is a normal and telltale indicator of a particular point in a learning process[1] you and your people are experiencing all the time. As a coach, I've helped so many leaders who were innocently missing or misreading the details of this process as everyone got really frustrated and performance tanked. By the end of this chapter, you'll understand exactly why these things occur, know what they mean, and have best next steps ready when you spot them again so you can accelerate your team forward.

First, we need a good visual of what's going on.

Let's take a drive...Imagine yourself driving on the highway. As you do, you peer over at the car and driver to your right, and another to your left. The driver to the left is laid back, listening to his stereo, chatting on his phone, sipping his coffee with one hand, relaxed and at ease. The driver to your right looks nervous, gripping the wheel with both hands, intently looking at the road, your car, his console and then the road. His radio is off, there are no passengers in the car and he's clearly concentrating hard on driving. Veteran driver vs. Newbie driver, right? You've been in both positions, and so have I. It seems like forever ago when you were a newbie driver with that kind of intensity, right? What happened between then and now was the gaining of competence and confidence, a formulaic process playing itself out right now in different contexts for everyone on your team with varying skill and talent areas. To decipher what's really going on in their competence, we'll stay with this driving example...

Stop for a minute and grab a sheet of paper. If you're on an airplane, a napkin will do. If you can, do it in the margin of this book. Draw the diagram[2] in your own notes as I build it here...

1. Cluelessness, UC

When you were five, you probably had no idea that there was even a distinction between standard shift and automatic shift, right? You just got in the car and someone took you to where you needed to be. So, regarding the skill of stick-shift driving, you were Unconscious Incompetent; you didn't even know (unconscious) that you didn't know how to do it (incompetent). And that was fine.

Ignorance is bliss, right?

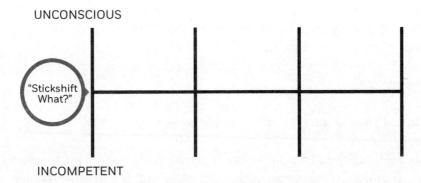

2. (possibly Rude) Awakening, CI

Then you got to be driving age. You decided you wanted to learn how to drive, maybe even a stick shift... You sat behind the wheel for the first time and instantly became acutely aware of how much you didn't know. If it was stick shift, then the car was stalling, jumping, and you felt like you were going to drop the transmission any minute. You thought you knew what you were doing a little, but the voice in your head was either screaming, "Wow—cool," or "You have no idea what you're doing—you suck at this!"

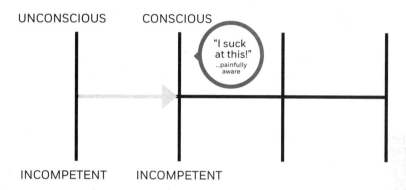

UNCONSCIOUS   CONSCIOUS

"I suck at this!" ...painfully aware

INCOMPETENT   INCOMPETENT

Welcome...You've arrived at Conscious-Incompetence. At this point you were no longer completely ignorant or blissful. You were definitely still Incompetent, but now *Consciously* so. That could be painful or inspiring—it depends on you, the situation and the voice/s in your head.

Jump out of this driving flashback for a moment and back into present time, with one of the people on your team who's clueless in one of those skills they need to learn and perform. There are two ways this can go:

1) Eager Beaver... Wide-eyed, eager to dive into what they haven't experienced or learned yet. They blink a lot, processing as fast as they can, might ask a lot of questions right away, consciously mapping the territory of what they have yet to learn.

2) Bubble Burst... Full of confidence without actual competence to back it up, they think they know a lot more than they really do. They get a rude awakening with real-life feedback (likely from you) to that effect, and in fact have a whole lot to learn, quickly. Ouch.

Either way, remember what it felt like to be behind the wheel that first time...scary, exhilarating, overwhelming, cool...a lot at one time. That's where your newbie is here. How it goes at this point is key, and can either accelerate the rest of the learning or grind it to a screeching halt. Here's why...

Downshifting

We have moments that cause our minds to flash-flood with unproductive emotions like fear, anger, panic or frustration. Realization that we really don't know what we're doing or are looking really bad[3] trying could be one of them, especially when exacerbated by our little voice freaking out in high critic mode. The more overpowering those negative emotions are, the more compromised our mental processing becomes.

Some neuroscientists aptly call this *downshifting*[4]; like driving a car in fifth gear at 70 mph, all systems firing. If we suddenly downshift to first gear, the engine simply can't go that fast and we'll burn up the transmission trying to force it. A blast of panic, fear or anger (like "Oh @#%!—I can't do this! I look really stupid! My boss is watching me flail right now!") downshifts you into the brain's first gear: survival mode. There, you can't access higher-order-thinking-skills as normal, and can't process anything beyond basic preservation by defending ourselves (fight) or bailing out of the situation (flight, which also manifests as shutting down). It's not pretty. It's the worst spot when there's learning or performance on the line, yet we've all been there. We've also all triggered it for someone else. The more you confront someone about how much they're NOT getting it the more likely they are to downshift, making it worse.

You might have someone on your team who's there right now, their thinking and ability to learn/perform completely crippled.

When downshifting occurs, the only antidote is to cool down enough for the brain to upshift back to full capacity. That's why you always think of your best comebacks hours after a big argument or confrontation. Your brain can't get to where the clever comebacks are (fifth gear) when you need them in the moment of conflict, because it downshifted into first gear, far away from that sophistication. Hence, you come up with those best retorts in hindsight, after you've regained thinking power. I'll give you more tools[5] for how to upshift yourself or someone else, but for now, just keep this phenomenon in mind and know that the best thing to do is keep the learning experience positive[6] and calm so you or that person can stay present, clear, firing on all cylinders of fifth-gear, higher-order thinking skills, learning forward. Be their supportive yet challenging coach, not their critic. Now, back to that diagram.

3. The Sweet Spot of Learning

If you're driving today, you stuck with it. You made it through that discomfort and kept practicing, but it was probably messy. One minute you had it, the next minute you didn't, and you weren't consistent for a while. The little voice hates this part because it wants you to always look good, and that's hard to do here because you're all over the place until you start to really get it.

The great news is that you can quiet the inner heckler, and turn up the volume on your inner positive coach. This phase can be awesome. And it is truly the sweet spot of learning. You're fully aware that you don't have it down yet, but really want to learn it, doggedly determined, hungry...the best!

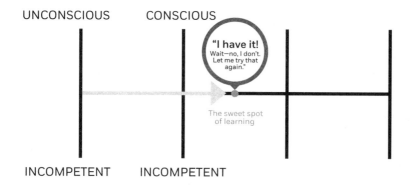

For your newbie in this spot, your role as their coach is important. If they're into it, it's a blast to coach someone here because they're wide open, sucking it in. But if they're getting nervous, showing signs of defensiveness or shutting down, pipe up your visible, audible support to drown out their little voice telling them they can't do it. You've been there yourself, so go back to your empathy as a fellow learner.

4. I Think I Can, CC

After a period of flailing, they can finally do this new thing, but it takes a lot of brainpower. The new driver is still gripping the wheel, unable to have the distractions of passengers or the radio yet. You may even need to cue yourself out loud as you do it: "Press in on the clutch, let up on the gas, then shift!"

So you're definitely driving (competent), yet definitely need hyper-focus to do so. It takes all of your consciousness to stay that competent.

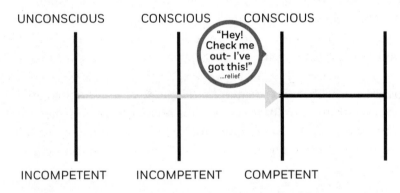

Finally the pieces come together. You can pull it off decently. You can drive with the radio on. Then you can have a passenger, and then you can talk about something else while driving. For your newbie learner, s/he can do this new thing without so much buildup beforehand or being so mentally exhausted afterward...at last!

On it!

For most things we need to do well, we get smoother, able to handle curveballs, and that deliberateness remains. We execute well, with intentionality to every part of it, which ensures its success and quality. This is solid Conscious-Competence, where we can crank out consistently solid results with great control. We're completely competent, aware of why, what, how and when we're doing it the whole time. Your solid, consistent performers are here, conscious to the point of conscientious.

5. Mastery, UC

As a driver, you got to the same place of that guy to the right of you on the highway. You sip your smoothie, cart passengers, listen to the radio and talk on your phone while driving, not even thinking about it, right? You became **Unconsciously Competent.**

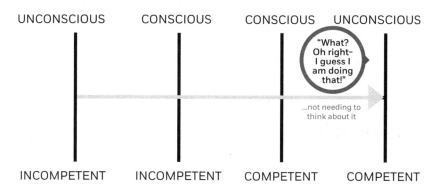

UNCONSCIOUS   CONSCIOUS   CONSCIOUS   UNCONSCIOUS

"What? Oh right- I guess I am doing that!"

...not needing to think about it

INCOMPETENT   INCOMPETENT   COMPETENT   COMPETENT

Coming back to real time and competence areas you're seeking or expecting others to master and excel in...this smoothness is what we're going for, right? With the right intention, this is when ease with speed, efficiency, excellence and range (as in competence even with unexpected challenges in the mix or within a diverse range of situations) expand. When someone's got that, we start dropping "the T word."

Talent

"Talent" is the way we reference how unconsciously awesome someone is at something, and we then compare, rank, and measure.

You've got lots of it on your team right now, both realized and potential.

This is a big topic in coaching, leadership and human performance. How someone becomes talented is important, and hotly debated. Is talent learnable? Is it not? I could share an equally significant stack of books from my shelf representing both sides of that learnable[7] vs. unlearnable[8] debate, but for our purposes here, let's just hold that there are two different kinds of talent in you and on your team—learned and natural.

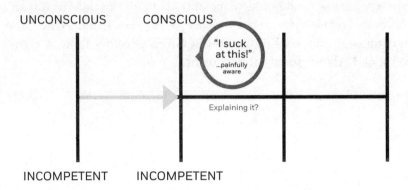

All talent is great. Learned talent is excellent. Natural talent is exceptional. I believe that peoplecan get to talent both ways, but inborn talent will always outperform learned talent when it's tested (by pressure and other x-factors) because it's the manifestation of hard-wired instinct defining our natural survival patterns. We finally have great diagnostics[9] and pinpoint-accurate vocabulary to describe different kinds of natural talent themes, which has opened up a whole new way for us to understand and accurately leverage inborn ability.

The Talent Brake
When you're unconsciously competent to the point of real talent, how do you explain how to do it to someone who's clueless? If you're a NASCAR driver, how do you suddenly teach someone who has never been behind a wheel before?

It's hard. You don't think about the steps of what you do anymore, so how can you explain them? This is what happens when we take a star who's so great that we've decided to have them train or supervise others. We think they'll keep accelerating forward, but then everything slows down. Maybe that happened to you when you first got people under you to manage. You knew how your reports should do something because you could do it easily, quickly and in your sleep. But could you teach it? Define success for it? Outline all the micro-steps to it? Uh oh.

Most leaders begin as talented contributors who excelled. We have a tendency to take people who are really skilled at something and unintentionally move them away from doing that something. We want to make their impact bigger, so we promote them to management or leadership of that something. A talented designer becomes a creative director, where they no longer design, but instead manage people who might not have talent anywhere close to their own. A gifted engineer is promoted to lead younger engineers. It happens in every industry, in every kind of job. And, in a way, it makes sense.

But it changes the game completely for them. It feels like slamming on the brakes when they were in cruise mode. All of a sudden, they're back to Conscious-Incompetence—not with the original area of performance, but with this new thing called training or leading someone else in what I don't even have to think about, which they don't know how to do.

The Natural Talent Mistake
This brake-effect is even worse with natural talent. When someone arrives on the scene with the innate ability to hit it out of the park right away, it's a beautiful thing. We're wowed, and they're psyched. There are few things more satisfying than doing what we do well instinctively AND it being the right fit for what someone else needs. It's a holy grail combination. Like Michael Jordan for the Bulls, a person at that level, left to their own devices, will outperform our expectations and thrive doing what they do best.

Unfortunately, we often make the mistake of elevating someone like that as the model for everyone else to meet AND the teacher/trainer/mentor for the wide-eyed newbies. MISTAKE! This move usually goes horribly. The superstar gets annoyed and feels slowed down, the newbies get intimidated because they feel they'll never get to that level (and few will), and not much valuable training actually happens. Because...

That *natural* superstar *started* at Unconscious-Competent, rather than learning their way to it. So they've never had consciousness to explain how or why they do what they do...they just know they can do it if you give them the right setup for it. So asking them to teach it is an exercise in frustration because they don't have words, steps or frameworks to break down what you're wowed by. The best trainers, mentors and coaches of anything are those who understand the nuance of what it takes to be awesome at something, AND can articulate, explain and teach it from the clarity of Conscious Competence. Michael Jordan learned how to lead and coach his teammates because Phil Jackson taught him how to bring Consciousness to his Competence and articulate it to his teammates as a captain. And your stars can get that too. NOW what?

Here's how to accelerate the process and leverage your talent into leadership:

You

You're talented at driving. But were you always? Nah, you learned your way there. In your professional life, you're pretty used to being smooth, not bumpy and messy so much anymore. Yet that's what might feel a bit here with this new area of competence- influencing or leading in this new way I keep proposing.

- **Give yourself space to go through the process and be a learner.** As you learn the concepts in this book, keep coming back to the UC-UI process, and remind yourself that you're in your own process (probably multiple ones at once).

- **Map your process along the way.** Throughout the book, chart your process and plot where each tool is and how it's moved in your competence. "Hey—check me out! I'm actually Unconsciously Competent now in addressing WIIFM all the time!" If you're reflective, keep track in a notebook the things you're trying, how it feels, what you're learning/tweaking, and what response you're getting.

- **Get perspective on yourself.** Intentionally pan out to see if you can spot your own unconscious-competent patterns as you lead, react and interact. The more conscious you are about what you're doing, the more intentional choice you have about the best next move rather than just going on auto-pilot all the time.

You With Them

They're in their own processes, which may or may not be moving at the pace you'd like. While it can feel like a roller coaster for them, your influence makes all the difference between a terrifying or awesome ride.

- **Empathize.** As you watch them clueless, stuttering, smoothing out or soaring, remember what it was like to be in those spots, your little voice screaming in your head. Slow your Unconscious-Competent self down to be patient with their process. What do you wish someone had told you, shown you or done for you?

- **Highlight the wins.** They may not see their own progress in the moment because they're so focused on what they still don't know ahead. So you be the one to call out progress. Even pros need the fans to celebrate every yard gained, not just the touchdowns.

- **Cheer.** While they're in the learning process, their little voice will mess with them. It's up to you to drown out their little voice with your support from the outside. Tell them it's okay for the roller coaster to lurch, that they've got it, that you believe in them.

- **Set up your Talent.** When you're considering stand-out rock stars of talent on your team for leadership, first ask yourself how they got there. Learned or Wired? The learned talent can get to consciousness quicker, since they were just there not so long ago. The naturals will have a bigger transition, so really assess where their ultimate best fit is before moving them. The naturals will have a bigger transition, so really assess their ultimate best fit before moving them. To get them to their next level of leadership, invite them into a process to become a leader—more Conscious about their Competence so they can lead others in it. Pair them with a hungry, strong CI learner with the directive of getting inside the star's head, noticing and documenting patterns in what they do naturally to find repeatable, teachable steps in what they do. They'll both learn!

You can help others take leaps forward in their process and mastery as you take on your own. That's your WIIFM. That's what you'll get out of all of what follows. You'll learn how to tap into your team's greatness, inspire them as a leader and make them better.

Trust me.

Notes:

"How often do you get to be the ultimate coach, able to create and find that greatness...where people can be even better, smarter than they might otherwise show up? "

Chapter 4:
Your Options

You'll need some different colors of pens for this chapter. I prefer the four-color click pen, but see what you've got. We'll be setting up many of the next chapters in these few pages, so go grab your pens now.

Think of a time in your life when you felt like a person of influence tapped into your greatness. Maybe it was a coach. Maybe it was a teacher. Maybe it was a relative. Maybe it was a boss. Maybe it was a mentor. Somebody who typifies, to you, the idea of the ultimate coach, who's able to reach inside you, pull out your brilliance and have you step right into it.

An instance or person might jump into your mind, but if not, it's worth it to your process to stop for a minute here and really think about it; reflect on leaders you've experienced and seen, and that feeling of stepping into your own greatness which someone else found or sparked for you. If you've never experienced someone's impact that way yourself, imagine what it would be like. Think about a leader who you've seen even from afar or in history and envisioned having that affect...or even one you wish existed.

Now that you've pinpointed that person, think about the characteristics that stood out. How would you describe the role they played for you?

You wear all kinds of hats during the day. Over the course of even a week, there are so many different roles that you play and juggle all the time. Sometimes you really are the manager, just keeping everything on the rails and moving forward. *Managing situations* is one thing, yet your people need you to *lead* them. So how often do you get to be that kind of influencer, leader, the ultimate coach, able to find their greatness and have that multiplier[1] effect where people can step up to be even better, smarter than they might otherwise? We're going to increase whatever frequency and capacity you have there, but first let's break it down a bit.

Think again of that ultimate influencer—all the characteristics it takes to be a person like that. You can zoom in of that specific person in your life, yet also imagine all the great coaches in the world and the leaders you aspire to be like, and tag them with one-word descriptors—adjectives to describe them or the roles they play. Could be things like patient, model, brave, courageous, fierce, empathic. Here are a few examples from influencers I think of often:

- Steve Jobs: visionary, powerful, uncompromising
- The Rev. Dr. Martin Luther King, Jr.: communicator, visionary, teacher, soul-searcher
- Oprah Winfrey: disarming, empathic, human, model, brave
- Ghandi: still-yet-strong, focused, deeply powerful
- Phil Jackson: Zen, grounded, holistic, multiplier, winner, expert, strategist

Take a few minutes to add to the list on the next page. Add any words that come to you as you think of the ultimate coach, leader or influencer. This page will come to be important and the most-referenced page in this book for you later on, so take your time here and leave a little space somewhere on the page to add a few more words as they come to you throughout.

> **Actually pause here to fill up
> the next page before you read on**

VISIONARY
POWERFUL
COMMUNICATOR
SOUL-SEARCHER
EMPATHIC
MODEL
BRAVE
RISK-TAKER
TRUTH-TELLER
MIRROR-HOLDER
QUESTIONER
BELIEVER
POSSIBILITY-HOLDER
HAMMER
TRAILBLAZER
MEASURER
PARTNER
ADVOCATE
AGILE
CALL-MAKER

STRATEGIST
UNCOMPROMISING
TEACHER
DISARMING
HUMANE
HUMAN
FOCUSED
STANDARD-SETTER
CHEERLEADER
RELENTLESS
CHALLENGER
ANALYST
SHARER
INSTIGATOR
FRIEND
BEACON
ORCHESTRATOR
FORECASTER
MEDIATOR
LISTENER

You're learning.

Nicely done.

Now, let's just compare that list with you as a leader on any given day. Here's the big question...
Are you all of those things as a leader?
If you answered "not exactly," or some version of "no," let me rephrase the question...

Have you had at least *a moment* of being each one of those at some time as a leader?
Of course you have!

So, then the answer to the original question should be "Yes, I am all of those things as a leader," because if you've had at least a moment of them all, then we know that you've got them in you somewhere. Now we just need to pull them up, out and kicked into gear when you really need them. Or present more consistently, right? Right. On our way...

As you look through those particular words, which ones jump out to you the most?

Possible
You probably see descriptors that you'd most love to be able to step into and embody all the time as a leader, just like those influencers you imagined, yes? These are not the things you're already great at, but ones that you'd love to embody if we could tap your brilliance as a leader in your best moments or attributes you'd have if you had already become the leader you've always wanted to be. As we go through the rest of the book, I'll guide you in different ways to channel a lot of these qualities seen in the most inspiring and motivational leaders; not just managers who get stuff done and get stuff out of people, but leaders who do that and make major impact in a positive way as people grow. To make the process most meaningful for you, it may help to think now of those influencers or legendary leaders you most admire, and pin down the descriptors that best capture their brilliance you'd like to

emulate. Look through your list and identify three different words—
*the three that strike you the most as what you'd like to exemplify or
be more of, important attributes worthy of aspiration.*

Mark those three words in one of your colors (green, preferably) right
now.

*What would the impact around you be if you were able to embody those
three distinctions on demand, consistently?*

Easy
Now let's zoom in on what's most accessible all the time—what's
already working. You're currently having impact as a leader, and there
are some definite patterns to how that's happening. So, look at the list
again, and this time pick out the three words that best describe you
most of the time as a leader. These are the Unconscious-Competent
ones, which you typically just are without thinking about it. These are
your default settings as a leader. It's always good awareness to walk
yourself from autopilot back to Conscious-Competence so you have a
clearer view of your own patterns and more self-aware choice at your
fingertips.

*Wouldn't it be great to expand this list, especially to include some of the
green ones you circled a few minutes ago?*

Challenge
Next, let's look at the bad news. Check out the list one more time, and
find (or imagine—they are likely *not* on there) the descriptors of you
on your worst days as a leader. These are the descriptors you're least
proud of, but that you know pop up in your unfortunate moments as
an influencer. I know this isn't the fun part, but being able to call it and
tell the imperfect (or even damaging) truth about ourselves is critical
so we can get it up in clear view, in order to do something about it and
consciously see other options going forward. The more visible
something is, the more control we can gain over it. That which stays
hidden or we try to avoid seeing keeps looming—running us in the
background. Get it exposed, out and handled.

With a new pen color (red, ideally), pick or come up with three of these bad-news descriptors, then cross them out (after you write them in if needed). To make you feel better, here are my least proud (and now mostly contained, thanks to TIG), not on the list:

~~**STEAMROLLER**~~
~~**SARCASTIC SNIPER**~~
~~**VINDICTIVE**~~

Imagine having complete control over your challenge traits, with the control and agility to always choose more effective options that keep everyone thriving.

Now that we've got all of that identified, you're thinking about what being a leader looks like, sounds like and feels like with a little more specificity than you were a chapter ago, yes?

Excellent. You're considering your options. We just got a baseline for where you are and what'spossible for you as a leader, to setup the rest of your growth process, in which I'll show you how to make that shift.

Here we go...

*Call it
own it
Move on*

Notes:

Leader
Model
counselor
*cheerleader
nentor
motivator

* hero
partner
mediator
coach
listener
example
~~therapist~~

influencer
collaborator
inspiration
visionary
driver
believer
facilitator
team player
change agent
innovator
supporter
confidante

connector
advocate
optimist
challenger
* agytator
inspiration
educator

Moody
Negative
Dismissive

"Changing the question gets to something deeper, broader and more activating – where influencers make their distinctive mark. They don't just get results, they have reach. They have pull from the inside out."

Chapter 5:
Impact Is ALL YOU

Have you ever noticed how three different people can execute the same steps in a plan but get wildly different results?

Have you ever had a moment recently of one of those "bad news" traits taking over and saying/doing something you regretted as a leader?

Have you ever been in the middle of a meeting and suddenly wondered what the point was?

In the last chapter, we identified the ideal, default and bad-news traits about you as a leader with some specificity. Now let's look at what you're *causing*.

First, some owning up.

As you lead, direct, strategize, delegate, and even manage, you clearly juggle a lot. You're the one ultimately responsible for your team's results. Whether business is awesome, horrible, volatile, inconsistent, inspiring or sketchy...it's on you. Got it. Yet it goes further than just being accountable for it all. You're actually causing more than you realize. Beyond the visible results you hit, how each person under you orients to the work, feels in the organization, produces at the top of their game (or doesn't) and brings energy to it is *also* on you. Consciously or not, you're already having impact on all of those things. You leave a wake behind you, visible to everyone else all the time, even when you're not intending it. Drop a stone[1] to get to the bottom of a pond, and the ripples it causes on the water's surface cause impact on the pond's edge, 90 degrees away from the direction of the stone's travel. You're a big stone now, so you cause big ripples. The bigger your position, the more it all counts. People hear what you say, watch what you do and pick up on where you are, usually magnifying it, good or bad. They then choose their path and interpretation of what it means as a result. That could be great, damaging or a missed opportunity multiple times per day. This may reassure or panic you. You might have a firm handle on it or be secretly hoping that it goes one way or another. Either way... what you're causing **counts**, *so let's get it right.*

There are a lot of models out there that link result to cause, desire to plan. I'm not here to teach you planning models—you can get those in a simple Google search. I'm committed to your impact getting bigger, more powerful and more intentional. To do that, we'll use a frame that's simple in concept, but huge in impact moment to moment.

1. Have

Like most leaders, you spend a lot of time talking about results. Your success is judged, competition monitored and team's success measured by them.

What rank did we end up with? What metric are we pushing for? What are the final numbers?

If your team doesn't know the result they're shooting for, they lose momentum, focus and direction. Without a clear finish line, no one will keep running faster. Got it. Really good managers make concrete results clear first. Yet great leaders look further than that, and you need to play a bigger game as an influencer. I'll assume that you already do a great job at outlining the specific deliverables or framing out the metrics expected by your constituents, yet how often do you drive deeper and broader—*beyond* those measurables? What if you asked the question a bit differently?

WHAT IMPACT DO I WANT TO *HAVE*?

Critically different from the question"What result am I going for?"-this is more than just semantics. Changing the question gets to something deeper, broader and more activating—where influencers make their distinctive mark. They don't just get results, they *have reach*, they *have pull* from the inside out, they have impact that creates intentional ripples of more and more impact. HAVE is the very first thing that every great influencer asks themself before they goes into any idea, plan, conversation, presentation, meeting and especially the office for the day. Yes, they call out specific results, but they also isolate all the other indicators that equal true impact.

Result only: *We want $XYZ in sales.*
Then ask yourself: *If we had that number, **what else** would we have?*
*We'd **have** a fired-up team,*
***have** buzz in the market,*
***have** people converting to our brand,*
***have** the street cred of solving what others couldn't*

Now we're talking about impact people can rally behind vs. a result for them to check off. As you broaden your thinking to have, it sets a bigger game and more meaningful orientation to it for everyone involved. Don't just hit results—have impact.

2. Do

So if the impact is on you, then how will you go about getting it once you identify it? How did you end up with the result you just got (even in your last interaction)? Every result and situation on your plate came from specific behaviors or actions that occurred in a particular way. *Every time.* I'm continually amazed by how many organizations and leaders harp on results without ever going deeper into the actual behaviors that cause them. Departments, initiatives and people are directed and evaluated to hit their results, yet there's little focus on how they'll hit them or what they did in the first place to miss their mark. Unfortunately, it can get skipped altogether, and someone is ranked or evaluated poorly (even demoted) based on their results, with no time spent on what caused it. They go forward with no learning, doing the same thing they've been doing (but hoping for different results), questioning their own ability and thinking they're just disliked by leadership. Craziness.

Behaviors create results.
We have to Do something different to create new impact.

So the next key question for the impactful leader is:

WHAT DO I NEED TO DO?

Now, let me point out a little difference between great leaders and frustrated ones in a classic scenario I've seen many times...

A leader of a particularly snarky and cut-throat young hotshot team identifies that he wants to *have* a team that's collaborating, seeking and giving one another feedback, supporting one another, feeling into what they're doing and really producing. He starts with "team culture" campaign posters on the walls and gives PowerPoint presentations about how everyone *should* try to behave. *And it doesn't work.* Because people are more intuitive than that, and will never authentically make those kinds of personal shifts just because someone told them to. We make shifts because we get *moved or inspired* to. If we're going to follow a leader in that way, it's only one who embodies what they're asking first.

Your people mirror *what **you** do* more than anything you *tell* them to do, so you've got to start way before you ask them to do anything.

That well-intentioned but ineffective leader with the PowerPoint made the mistake of asking the wrong *Do* question. He asked, "What will **they** need to do in order for 'team' to happen?"

To **Have**...	A true team that's collaborating, seeking and giving one another feedback, supporting one another, feeling into what they're doing and really producing
What I need to **Do** as a leader	• Model. • Reframe the way that I think and approach the team. Watch the way that *I* speak to people. • Hold the snark and judgment. • Focus on what's possible and positive. • Ask for feedback. If I want them to ask one another for feedback, they need to see me asking for feedback. • Visibly acknowledge and reinforce behavior that great teams do, like when they do cooperate that way, give feedback, when they do support one another. • Then... *later*... invite them to try it out with me.
??	

An influencer leader clarifies that, but only along with what *they* need to do themselves. If it went a little more like this flow, we'd see things-shift.

Your turn:

• *Get specific*

Going into an interaction, once the impact you want to Have is clear, ask yourself what you'll specifically need to Do to make that happen. Say what? Provide what? Model what?

• *You first*

What they need to do may be immediately obvious. Hold that aside for a moment and ask yourself what you as an Influencer need to model, do, cause or facilitate first in order for them to be able to do those things.

• *Get to the source before you move on*

When looking at a result that didn't go as planned, step back to the behaviors that caused it. What happened? Who did what when? How did they do it? This isn't about laying blame, but about getting to true cause, so you know what to change and **do** differently to **have** a different outcome next time.

•*Debrief*

At the midpoint and end of initiatives, projects or processes, get clear on what you Have and what you need to Do next. What do we have now? What worked? What didn't?

Real Influencer Moment:

For our chef, he had to really look at his behaviors as a leader and what needed to change for the environment he created to be fun. He made a whole plan for himself of things he personally would need to do differently since he was typically driving folks pretty hard with an edge to him a lot of the time.

So...he set up a joke of the day, started games with his line cooks, had the wait staff get into it by coming in to just tell them how much they were appreciated or bringing them smoothies in the middle of a big push...things which would spark exactly what he wanted to have: a fun environment. He also had a whole list of what he personally had to do every single day to make sure he was bringing it- like playing really fun music as he got the day started, leading cheers when he knew his own energy might be lagging, coming in with great nutrition, having worked out already to make sure that he had enough energy all the time...

What do we want to **do** differently?

3. Be

This is the game-changer. And the part most leaders miss completely. We think that once the plan of attack is set, it's just about executing it to get the desired result. But it's not. Don't get me wrong—I'm very strategic, and value all mapped and alternatives paths to the goal as critical. But there's more to it.

Even more powerful than what you're **do**ing is what comes before any of that, which could be sabotaging the whole thing for you as a leader. You've had interactions and initiatives in which you did the right things, even said the right things, but didn't get the impact you wanted, right? I certainly have.

In those moments of frustration we get in our own way because coloring everything we do or say is *who we're **BEing***.

That is... who are you mentally, emotionally and physically *being* at the moment? What attitude or mindset are you in? We all have countless versions of ourselves that we end up BE-ing at any moment. This is where your list of options from chapter #4 comes back in. Look again at your patterns, and what else is possible on that list from the greats. Those are all BE options for you, any time. Most people default to the same few over and over (as you called out yourself), rather than the impact-creating versions of themselves they *could be* because they simply don't have the awareness you're now starting.

If our chef played out his whole new "fun atmosphere" game plan while **be**ing an *Impatient Bully*, it would fail, right? If you're being negative and judgmental in the meeting, but expecting others to openly share their ideas collaboratively, you're wasting your time because who you're **be**ing has already shut it down before you've even begun.

So...that impact and what ultimately occurs really *is* all on you.

The crux of it all for an Influencer comes down to Question #3:

WHO DO I NEED TO BE?

It's the crux because even with the most inspired vision of what I want to *Have* and best plan of what I need to *Do*, who I'm **Be**ing will determine how it actually goes.

One size definitely does not fit all when it comes to the people you need to influence. At various points, you may need to **be** the bottom-line-truth-teller, then the cheerleader, then the strategist, then the calming partner—all within a few hours. So, for every one-on-one conversation, the greatest influencers pause first to ask themselves, "What do I want to have out of this conversation? What am I going to do and who am I going to need to be?" The best do that in nanoseconds. They ask: Have? Do? Be? Then they step right into it: Be —> Do —> Have!

To start getting a handle on who you're BEing:
- *Own it*
  Now that you're thinking about who you're *Being* in a different way, pay attention to which version of you shows up moment to moment. It may be reactive or even leftover from who you were Be-ing in the meeting beforehand. Reflect on the last conversation you had, and call out who you were Be-ing and how that impacted the whole thing. "I was being impatient." "I was *being* a partner."
- *Choose ahead of time*
  Pause yourself before your next interaction. Think about what impact you want to *Have* here, what you'll need to *Do* to have that, and what version of yourself you need to *Be* to make it happen.
- *Use your menu*
  As you react to your world all day, you keep going to your default ways of being because you haven't expanded your repertoire yet and can't think of "listener"when you're in the moment of "taskmaster." Keep your list of ideal options from page 51 handy.

The best influencers go through mini versions of BeDoHave many times per day, can shift who they're **Be**ing quickly, and set everyone else up to get to their best versions too.

All Together.

Have "What impact do I want to have at the end of this?"	A true team: collaborating, seeking and giving one another feedback, supporting one another, feeling into what they're doing, producing	A fun environment with a kitchen staff of people who have fun all of the time while cranking in their quality of results: productive, effective and happy despite the slams of pressure	Collaboration with my partner (who's been combative)
Do "What will I need to DO to have that impact?"	• Model • Reframe approach to the team • Cut snark/judgment • Focus on possible & positive • Ask for feedback • Visibly acknowledge and reinforce true team behavior • Then...***after all that***... invite them to try it out with me	• Start day with fun music • Lead cheers when his own energy lags • Have great breakfast and workout before work • Start joke of the day • Start games with his line cooks • Get wait staff into it by coming in to tell them how much they are appreciated or bringing them smoothies in the middle of a big push	• Really listen with full attention • Imagine and try on every idea she's saying • Allow uninhibited connections, build on them • Communicate ideas about how we can work together • Keep body language open, relaxed, full eye contact.
BE "What version of myself do I need to BE in order to do that effectively?"	Supportive teammate	Funmeister	Partner

Plan this way → → →   *Act this way* ↑ ↑ ↑

You can choose what version of you as a leader shows up with intentionality, to make all the difference in the ripples you're causing.

Every single time.

Let's set it up.

BE.
DO.
HAVE.

BE.

DO.

Notes:

HAVE.

Broader

What else?

DEEPER

plan: example
      mentor
      cheerleader

"The small percentage of people who consistently outperform everyone else lock into the version of themselves they need to be, every time.
...Because they set themselves up for it, every time."

Chapter 6:
Setting Yourself Up

How do athletes get into their zone every time?
Why do most people abandon their resolutions early in the year?
How are certain leaders able to BE the best version of themselves even when things are falling apart?

"Be" is where we see great influencers taking a different path from the rest. Not just in big scenarios, but also before individual conversations —they stop, assess who they're **be**ing in the moment (could be a default, or a reactive bad-news trait, or leftover from who they needed to be in a meeting two hours ago), and consciously choose who they need to *Be* in the present moment for maximum impact.

To **be** *different from who you've been...*
Is it as simple as just deciding "I need to be open" and then I'm suddenly open when I've actually been pretty defensive in the previous five conversations? Not quite.

Being the specific, ideal version of yourself sometimes takes a little setup. It's not that you're having a personality change or that you throw out who you've been, but often you *are* going to tap a different part of yourself, possibly somewhere on that list you made earlier, far away from who you're already being in the moment.

Let's go back to the chef from the last chapter. The impact he wanted to *have* transforming the atmosphere and results of his kitchen were clear.
What he needed to *do* was really clear, from his own steps before he even walked in each morning to what he would do on the line.

Next, he had to get clear about his attitude or mindset—who he needed to *be* to pull it off. 'Funmeister.' That's how he captured the version of himself he knew he needed to be, a combination of instigator, model and cheerleader.

Now, notice that while we **plan** it from the ultimate impact we want to *Have*, then backfill what to *Do* and who to *Be*, in actually **playing it out**, you have to start from the beginning with who you're being. Think about the situation you've got going on right now. What fits best?

"I know I need to be a partner right now. But I'm not there at all—I'm just defensive with him every time we work together. Now what?"
That's real.

You also identified characteristics as *Possible* on your options page (51), ones you know would get you closer to being the leader you know you could be, but aren't as easy for you, and keep eluding you especially when you're pushed.
That's also real.

Even if you haven't seen the *Be* you know you need in quite a while, you know you've got it in there somewhere, right?

Not feeling it? Go out of order.

Maybe you know you need to *be a partner* with the person you're typically defensive with. That's rough, but common. Here's when you mess with the Be-Do-Have frame a level deeper to manually get yourself there. It's been said that "It's easier to act your way into feeling than feel your way into acting," and it's true. Sometimes it takes pulling up and out of yourself and the moment to imagine someone else who typifies the quality you're going for. What might we observe them doing in your situation different from what you're doing? What would you be doing if you were them? Then have a little coaching conversation with yourself. It might sound like this, the present defensive you talking to the possible you...

You start *out of normal order* with the easiest of the three parts—consciously *do*ing those things with some intentionality toward really becoming a partner, behaviorally jumpstarting your way into who you need to Be.

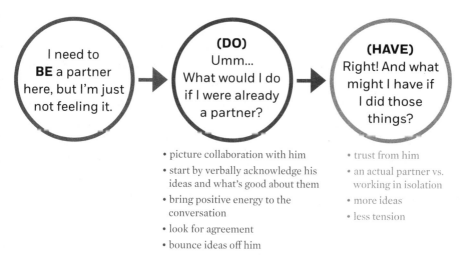

I need to **BE** a partner here, but I'm just not feeling it.	**(DO)** Umm... What would I do if I were already a partner?	**(HAVE)** Right! And what might I have if I did those things?

• picture collaboration with him
• start by verbally acknowledge his ideas and what's good about them
• bring positive energy to the conversation
• look for agreement
• bounce ideas off him

• trust from him
• an actual partner vs. working in isolation
• more ideas
• less tension

This works to switch gears and access it in the moment, often in a forced time-out[1] for yourself when you notice those troublemaking mindsets take over.

And sometimes it takes more than that...

Set it up
How do you consistently access the version of yourself you know you need to Be when it's just not intuitive yet?

Further-reaching than in the moment, you know that you've got those *Possible* traits from your listthat you want to **be** more consistently, right? To wipe out your challenge traits and *become* that list of awesomeness there's one more piece to this. It's the part that hardly ever comes up in goal-setting conversations, yet the reason that some people are consistently successful vs. everyone else who is not: *Conditioning.*

You've already got conditioning around you all the time, but it may be accidental. Places, smells, sounds, peopleall act as triggers[2] you don't even notice, sending you into versions of yourself that may be awesome or may be slowing you down. A certain song comes on the radio and you are fired up. You see a certain person's name pop up on your caller

ID, and you become sweet and charming. Someone brings up a certain topic, and you're instantly impatient and defensive.

Then there's very deliberate conditioning in your world. Your favorite TV show has never changed it's theme song because every time you hear it you become exactly what those producers want you to *be* as the show opens—attentive, pumped, inspired, maybe in suspense a bit, receptive. They chose that song very purposefully to that end. It's a setup. It's conditioning. And it works, every time.

Successful achievers and great, intentional leaders set themselves up *that* intentionally and consistently, and you can too.

We see the most obvious examples of this in sports. Some of the world's most elite athletes have very specific things as their Conditioning, to be exactly where they need to be mentally, emotionally and physically before performance time...

Dennis Rodman cycled on a bike before every game.
Shawn White listens to specific music before every run to be who he needs to be to break snowboarding records.
Cristiano Ronaldo has to get a fresh haircut before every game, and be the first person onto the pitch from his team.
Tiger Woods wears red shirts to compete when it counts (especially on Sundays).
Michael Jordan wore his lucky UNC basketball shorts under his Bulls uniform for every NBA game.
Rafael Nadal takes a cold shower exactly 45 minutes before every match.

Who do you need to *be* and what will guarantee you get there every time?

Let's take a look at something everyone can identify with: getting in shape. It's the most common New Year's resolution and the most-often abandoned as well.

We get clear on what we want to HAVE: desired weight (or XX pounds less), more energy, increased strength and stamina. We understand what's necessary to *do* behaviorally (diet and exercise). There are entire publishing industries propped up by diet books alone. Flip on the TV on a Saturday morning and you're inundated by exercise programs. It's not a lack of information on what to do that keeps us from shedding pounds. So we join the gym, make a plan, work out a few times, pay attention to what we're eating... Yet most people fail. Even when we know full well what to *do*. Why?

Because we cheat on the diet. We skip the gym. What's that about?

People let themselves off the hook and quit doing what they know they need to do because they allow themselves to be versions of themselves that don't work.

Being lazy.
Being an excuse-maker.
Being lenient.
versus
Being focused.
Being an athlete (if I were being an athlete, I wouldn't even question this workout—I'd already be doing it).
Being a coach to themselves.

In any of those last four[3], I'm on it, going for it, getting myself out the door to do my personal work, no question about next steps every day.

The small percentage of people who consistently outperform everyone else kick into the versions of themselves they need to be every time. ... because they **set themselves up for it,** every time.

Left to my own devices, I know I can get distracted or lazy vs. focused and relentless, and might not work out every morning, which I know I need to *do* in order to have the impact and health I want to *have*.

So I set up triggers for who I'll need to be; tripwires to get me relentless about it.

- My running shoes go on the edge of the bathroom sink before I go to bed so I have to pick them up before I brush my teeth in the morning.
- A post-it note like this goes on the bathroom mirror.
- Only healthy food replaces everything else in my fridge and pantry.

ATHLETE RUNNER RELENTLESS

- My favorite fired-up song is set to wake me up in the morning from my phone.
- I might have a running partner I've committed to, who won't let me skate out of it.

The tech world now gets the power of conditioning. Fitbits™ and other wearables condition us to be more aware of our movement and activity. Tools like mint.com send you reports of your current spending in categories so you'll be more conscious as you spend. You can get an alarm clock that not only makes a sound to wake you up, but physically hurls itself off your nightstand and wheels itself around the room so you have to get out of bed and chase it to turn it off. That's conditioning to be awake every morning!

Let's go back to our chef, who set himself up:

To be the Funmeister every single day, he asked himself what conditioning he could set up to be that *no matter what* else was going on, even if the pressure was on, before his employees walk into that kitchen? He create a role for a *partner-* Funmeister with him, which rotated on the team. Getting to be the Funmeister with him became a coveted role on the team, so every single day there was somebody different ready, anticipating, ideas churning, signed up.

He would meet them before the shift started and they'd get one another fired up as Funmeisters with music, jumping around, jokes, creating a game for the day and that became conditioning for him to get and stay there every day.

Knowing your easiest triggers, how can you *set yourself up* to *be* those possible traits? Some Conditioning ideas, each to set up ahead of time...

Have a reminder (voice or visually) pop up on your phone every morning to ask you the following before you workout or shower:
• What's the horizon you're working toward?
• What's possible that hasn't been done before?
• What's the really big picture?

Write "VISION FIRST" on a post-it note to go on your computer... as a reminder to begin every communication to your team with the big picture of where this can ultimately lead...

Get a whiteboard up in your workspace... and use it to map your ideas as big as possible.

BE...
The Visionary

Write "THINK BIGGER" or "10, 20, 50 YEARS FROM NOW" on post-its, an place in key places around workspace...

Schedule weekly ideation time on your calendar, as important as other appts. Protect it.

Have someone on your team be the vision questioner... to keep asking you about it- it will force you to keep articulating it until it gets smooth

Spend time with a visionary... Create a regular touchbase with him/her about what you each have going on. Follow his/her cues or patterns of creating and communicating scope and long-range impact.

You'll notice that these are all things that you don't have to go seek out in the moment (because you won't). They are *preset tripwires* you run into on your way to doing everything else, and that's why they work. So... what are you going to change in your environment? What support are you going to set up for yourself to BE the leader you know you can be more consistently and powerfully?

Some easy conditioning...

Visual Tags
• Write the word that best captures who you want to BE in the palm of your hand. You'll see it all day long as a reminder.
• Place sticky notes of key phrases/questions to trigger who you want to BE in key places—on your bathroom mirror, rear-view mirror in the car, etc.

- Make the wallpaper of your phone and computer visual reminders of who you can be.
- Find a photo or image that captures you *being* that version of you. Make it your phone wallpaper and put it up in your workspace.

Auditory Clues

- Record yourself a voicemail that will inspire you to BE that version of yourself, and save it. Listen to it over and over.
- Find a song that signals that version of who you can BE, like a theme song. Make it the last thing you listen to before you head into your day of leading.
- Craft the perfect WIIFM question that will ring true for that version of yourself, and post it all over in key places you'll see it and ask yourself.
- Talk with someone about who you'd like to BE as a leader more intentionally. Vocalizing it will give it more reality.

Kinesthetic Taps

- Grab a partner. Find a person who's able to nudge you into this version of yourself easily, and will keep checking in with you about it.
- Find a physical momento from an experience in which you were being this version of yourself. Keep it in your pocket or workspace.
- Notice which clothes in your closet make you feel like this version of yourself. Wear them when you want to BE that, and buy more of them.
- Get yourself moving—walk, run, get yourself physically there. Create a power move to anchor that version of yourself (think the "Yesssss!" motion from *Home Alone*).

Once you start setting yourself up, *being* who you need to *be* isn't nearly the crapshoot it is for everyone else all the time. You know who you need to be, and you step right into it, supported by your conditioning.

That's you, tapping your own greatness on demand.
Give it a try and see how it works.

Notes:

Halftime Review

We've covered a lot so far. Stop here for a moment and take some time to digest what you've taken in so far.

Reflect on each of the chapters you've read.

Go through each one, read the notes you made in the margins and on your note pages, and write new ones.

Play with the concepts. Test them through the lens of your real life—each piece that you have gone through, learned, tried out in your own world and now are honing and tweaking and perfecting on your way to mastery as you added these pieces into your repertoire as a leader.

Put the concepts into your own words. Create the 'elevator' version, a summary of what we've covered that you can explain to someone quickly, concisely and with meaning.

We have a lot more to cover in the second half of this book. It's important, before you proceed, to feel comfortable with what you've read so far.

I've left a blank page here for you to make notes on.
<--

Spend some process time and then come back for the second half.

"...it's so much faster to just tell them, isn't it? But don't. Because if you just give them the answer (again) a few things happen..."

Chapter 7:
Coaching Them to Impact

I'm betting you can relate to one of these:

You give feedback or even a full review (year, quarterly or even end-of-project) for somebody, then expect them to take it, run with it and create an action plan for improvement, achievement and awesomeness. **But they don't.**

Or...

*You end up spelling out the new results they need to hit, AND creating their plan of execution **for** them? You walk away wondering, "Will they really get there?" Or even, "If I hadn't laid all that out, would they have ever come up with it themselves?"*

Enough of that. What if you could give the feedback, and then *they* come up with an awesome plan for impact forward out of it—including everything down to setting themselves up with the right conditioning to be who they need to be?

Completely possible. Now that you know how to set *yourself* up to have the kind of impact you are ultimately going for, we can get your people there, too.

First, let me just call something out. You know in your heart of hearts that it's better to get them to come up with their plan than it is to just give them the answers. Yet you don't. Probably because you haven't had a great way to do it effectively, consistently or quickly. Now you will.

We just convert it into a process you coach your people through to generate their own impact. With this process, you'll be able to simply ask the right questions for them to create the ideas, strategy, motivation and setup they'll be psyched to take on.

When it comes time to execute, we know that we work from the Setup forward, but to map it all out we start with the end in mind first, right? So it's simple (in concept). We turn each step into a question for them to answer and come up with their own plan.

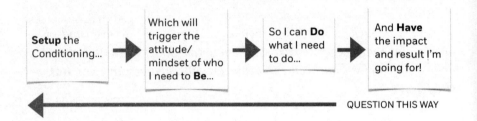

Step 1: They own their impact

With that wide-eyed (if they have an idea without a plan) or squinty-eyed (if you just gave them feedback) player across from you, take a deep breath, get clear on who you need to BE (the ultimate positive coach, tapping into their ability to have huge impact), and start at the top.

> "So, what impact do you want to **have** in this area that you aren't having yet? What result would you like to get that you don't have right now?"

You ask and then you wait.

That's the weird part, and for some of us the hardest part. We're so used to having the answer already for them (you had it in your head before the conversation even began), and so are they. And it's so much faster to just tell them, isn't it? But **don't**.

Because if you just give them the answer (again) a few things happen:

1. **They don't own it.** It's your idea not theirs. It's just one more thing you created or assigned. Everyone's a legend in their own mind, and like their own ideas better than anyone else's.

2. **They don't have to engage or think**. Why bother if you're going to

lay it all out for them anyhow?

3. **They stay dependent on you for the answer.** The more you feed them the lines, the more they just wait for you to create the next plan, passive instead of active, initiating or doing the work to create their own path. Over time, they lose trust in their own ability to create impact.

The power of it coming out of their mouth vs. yours is immeasurable. It's not that your goals for them aren't critical, but we want them *to own it* enough to articulate themselves what they're going to accomplish, and what impact they'll create. Now they will.

So, shhh. Ask the question, and wait for them to think.

They may get uncomfortable, and give you a searching-for-the-right-answer face, silently (or audibly) asking, "What do you want me to say?" It might take a little adjustment on both your parts to NOT give them the answer, so rephrase to get them going: "You tell me. What results/impact are you getting or not getting now versus the result or impact you *want to have*?" Then allow them to come up with the answer.

Once they come up with something, you get to help them refine it super specific and awesome. What's it going to look like? What's it going to sound like? What's it going to feel like?

Let's say a retail regional field leader (with 15 districts under her) is talking with a district leader (with 15 stores under her) about customer service:

RL: "So, what impact do you want to have in customer service?"
DL: "Well, I want all of my stores and their staffs to really prioritize customer service and have better customer service interactions."
RL: "Okay, great. Write that down! What impact would it have on the rest of the business for them to prioritize and have better customer service interactions?"
DL: It would create great experiences for our guests."
RL: "Great. Jot that down, too. What impact would that have?"

DL: It could increase guest trust, loyalty and even their dollars spent per sale.

RL: Great. Jot that down, too. What impact would that have?

You get the idea here. By simply asking that question deeper and deeper, we direct their thinking into really specific ripples of impact and ultimate results they could have.

Now here's the key... Notice that after every part of the answer, we're cueing them with "Great, write that down." *They're* writing it in their own notes vs. you writing it in some performance plan for them. That sends a very clear message, which is ***this is for you, not for me.***

Step 2: They map their path

Once they get all the specificity of the Impact they'll have down, ask...

"Great! So What will **you** need to do to make that happen? What will you need to start or try or take on?"

If you get another curious face, add onto the questions with all the parts you know it'll take for them to really have that impact they're going for.

*What needs to **happen** to really have that impact you just identified?* (she answers, writes it down)
*What **steps** will that take?* (answer, write)
*What will you need to **do that's** different from what you've been doing?* (answer, write)
*What conversations will you need to **have**?* (answer, write)
*What meetings do you need to **put together**?* (answer, write)
*What campaigns do you need to **start** in order to get that impact you want?* (answer, write)
*What new behaviors might you need to **model** for your team?* (answer, write)

An important piece here is focusing them on what they need to do, not what their people need to do. As it was for you, that'll be a shift for them in influence as a leader. You'll guide it by asking those questions until you know they've got a solid plan that will get the impact.

So, our district manager might come up with a plan for how she's going to model, teach, talk to her team about and kickoff a campaign for customer service—all things we could've laid out for her, but would've gone in one ear and out the other. She came to them on her own because her boss asked the right leading questions, and gave her enough confidence and space to actually come up with the answers.

Yes, and...

It's important that as they comes up with ideas in this part that you're encouraging, and not squashing any of their ideas. If it's just an okay idea (and you know it could be better) say, "**Yes! And** what else could you do? What have you seen other folks with that impact do?" This is a technique from improv comedy that is invaluable in leadership. If someone steps into a sketch with me on stage, their job as a co-performer is to keep the momentum going and *build* from what I just put out there. "Yes, and..." is the go-to phrase to keep it moving forward and give my brain enough time to finish that sentence in a way that builds.

Specificity

If she says, "Oh, I need to have some meetings," say, "Great. What kind of meetings do you need to have? Who are the key people who need to be at those meetings?" "How are you going to kick off the meetings?" "Okay, and when will you need to have them? How many of them are you going to have?" "Okay, good. Write that down." This is right about when the person you're coaching starts to get excited about their own idea. They start writing faster as the ideas flow. As you spark ideas with your questions, they are the one who's creating it, and that's the power.

Step 3: They get their head in the game

Once they come up with that list of very specific behaviors—
their plan of attack—you cross them over to that world of the
unfamiliar for average folks, yet guaranteed impact for the best leaders
and achievers...

> "Awesome.
>
> What attitude or mindset will you need to
> **be** in to do all of that you just came up with
> really well and really consistently?"

This might be the part that stumps them the most at first. *You* now
understand the power of BE, but they have no idea... yet. So you ask
it again, as they start to understand: *"We all get thrown off easily—so
what attitude or mindset will you need to have in order for to do all of
those things you just listed consistently, with energy, in a time frame that
works, and to have the impact and result you want?"*

They might say something like "I need to have a positive attitude?"
Because that's about the extent of most people's vocabulary when it
comes to who they're BE-ing.
Be patient with them—you were there just a few chapters ago.

So, you might suggest a few. Again, you're not answering the question
for them, but you're giving them a menu to get it going. If you give the
brain a menu of options to pick from, it will either choose the right one
or it'll kick it into deductive mode to find the right one. I like to give
three suggestions—two that I think might be right, and one that is
definitely wrong (contrast works wonders to help the brain decipher).
*"Okay, do you think you need to be the <u>motivator</u> as you roll this out?
Maybe their <u>partner</u>, like in the trenches with them? Or the <u>tyrant</u>?"*
They'll either say, "Yeah, that's it," or, "No, I don't think that's it. I need
to be this...

Make sure that whatever they choose is not a big, lengthy thing. The
power of getting the right mindset for BE is in the brevity; we want it
to be a word or a phrase. If it's not one that they can say and have some

energy behind it, then it's probably not the right one, so you might want to have them try on different ones until they get one that really resonates.

And then, of course, "Great. Write that down!"

Step 4: They set themselves up

This is where they'll really have to think, because it's almost definitely not a piece that comes up in typical goal setting.

"Great, you've got the impact you're going to have all set, the plan all mapped, who you need to be to make it happen. Now... What support, tripwires or cues can you *set up now* all around you so you can *be that version of yourself*- get into that attitude or mindset easily and hold on to it consistently no matter what?"

So, notice I didn't use the word "conditioning" when I asked the question. I said, "What support will you need?" which you know is the same thing, but in their language. Again, the curious face and again you will offer a menu to get them started.

"Would it help to have a partner with this? Are there particular phrases that maybe you want to put on a post-it note and have in your car to trigger who you know you need to be? Is there something you could look at, maybe an inspirational quote or an image that triggers that part of you? Where can you put that? How about particular music that gets you in the right mindset? Where can you set it up so you hear it every day? What would help from me to get you there? How can you set these things up ahead of time so you can just run into them like tripwires?"

And then have them get it clear. Have them get really specific with things that they can do and set up for themselves. For each one you of course say, "Excellent! Write that down!"

By the end of this conversation, they've created a grand plan
for themselves of how they're going to truly have impact—not just another forgettable goal conversation where you churn out
metrics for them to hit and action steps to take, only to be
repeated a month later.

Now you can be the true coach setting them up rather than the taskmaster who came up with one more assignment.

Smooth!
So is there WIIFM in this approach? Absolutely, because it's all about
them, having phenomenal success, on their own power, in their own
terms. Total control over their own success. That's what we're going
for.

Disclaimer
This approach will take longer than you think it should the first time you
do it, because you're not used to asking the questions instead of giving the
answers. They aren't used to being so on-the-hotseat to create something
themselves. Neither of you are used to having some wait-time to actually
think about and come up with answers. Yet soon, they'll be coming to you
with their plan all the way down to the setup, and you get to just help them
tweak it. How awesome will that be-- to actually be able to coach them to
greatness instead of doing it for them? This really turns the ownership and
the power over to them, allowing them to tap into what's possible. So it will
take a little patience on your part in the beginning, totally worth it. Think of it
as front-loading your time and energy. What it takes to get comfortable with
it the first few times, you make up later as they create their own plans
on their own, crushing it.

**So, give yourself some space to get comfortable with the model.
It's going to get easier as you go.**

Here's how...
• *BE the coach*
   It would be really easy to take someone through this whole process
   being impatient (as you wait for them to get it) or maybe
   condescending (often comes with impatient), which would defeat the
   purpose of it, making it an exercise in drawn-out belittlement for

them. Watch for that. Intentionally BE the ultimate coach, committed to their success, pulling out their greatness and ideas, believing they can have huge impact, encouraging them. That makes it an ideation session for their greatness. Way better.

- *Cheatsheet*
The first time you do it, you might even have a sticky note that has a little cue for yourself for the questions in order, so you stick to it and don't start telling answers.

- *Empower*
Having them write it down (not you) is key to having them own it. So at the end of the conversation, say, "Great. Now that whole plan you just wrote, that's for *you*, not me. If you want to make me a copy of it, so that I can support you even better, that's great, but this is for you to have success, not for me to be checking up on you."

- *Support*
Make sure they know that you're supporting them beyond this conversation. At the end of it, say, "Great. So, when do you want to check back about this to see how you're doing and how I can support you even more? How about a week? How about two weeks?" Again, have *them* choose it.

- *Power of three*
The first time you do it, it'll be bumpy. The second time it'll get a little more comfortable. Unanimously leaders tell me that by their *third* conversation like this, the words get smoother, the questions more spot-on. Your people need three rounds, too. The second time you do this process with them (about some other result) it'll go twice as fast because you've already wired those question-lines in their heads, and they'll anticipate them a little, coming up with answers faster. By the third time, they'll be answering the questions before you even ask. Front-loading your time and energy!

Now you're coaching to influence their thinking... not managing!

Take a quick photo of this page to keep in your phone, so you can pull it up as a quick reference and cue for your next coaching conversation!

Ask...

1. "What impact do you want to **have**?

Layers: "What else?" "Then what will you have?" Go broad and deep.)

2. What will **you** need to **do** to make that happen?

("what else?" "then what will you have?" Go broad and deep.)

3. What mindset will you need to **be** in to do that?

(Give some menu options... *"Maybe the* motivator *as you roll this out? Maybe their* partner, *like in the trenches with them? Or the* tyrant?")

4. What support, tripwires or cues can you **set up now** all around you so you can *be that version of yourself–* get into that attitude or mindset easily and hold on to it consistently no matter what?

(Make VAK suggestions: sticky notes, voicemail to themself, screensaver photos, anchor object that takes them back to that State quickly)

Notes:

"If your people never see you stepping out, they never get a model or see you as human, and don't feel permission to do it themselves..."

Chapter 8:
Playing Bigger

#1 Let's go back to a moment in your life...

You're about to take the step, and never have before. Nobody knows how huge this moment actually is except you, because you're the one feeling your heart race, pores sweat, butterflies flapping in your stomach. Every fiber of your body is on red-alert. It's loud inside your head; your little voice is screaming at you, cajoling you, trying to reason with you... pulling out every trick it knows to get you to STOP. Decision time.

The last moment you had like *that* may have defined you. Because whether or not you took that step, whatever happened afterward, either opened something up or shut something down, which is why you'll remember it forever.

#2 Try this: Put the book down, cross your arms, and then come back. Great. Now do that again, except this time cross them the other way (other arm on top this time). That felt weird, right? You wanted to cross them back the first way, didn't you?

Welcome to your comfort zone.
You've heard of it before. We throw that term around and even joke "no thanks, that's outside my comfort zone. "Yet I wonder if you've got in-the-moment awareness of its bounds or have been able to take on how your existence in, out or teetering on the edge of your comfort zone is actually defining the depth, breadth and possibility of your impact every day more than you realize.

Let's quickly dismantle it first...

Your comfort zone is drawn as a box, yet in reality is more like a big bubble that surrounds you, going with you wherever you go. But mentally, developmentally and metaphorically, it's definitely a box that holds all the things you are used to, comfortable with, unconsciously competent at doing and generally unfazed by.

Of the following categories, you have quite a lot that falls both inside and out of your CZ:
• **People** (some folks on your team are in there, others are not)
• **Places** (even as specific as the certain spot on my couch I sit on every night)
• **Activities** (you might be okay bike-riding, not okay dancing)
• **Ideas** (some fit instantly, others are "too out there")
• **Emotions** (some you're okay showing regularly, others you avoid)
• **Food** (how often do you order the same thing at a restaurant?)
• **Clothes** (you have perfectly fine clothes in your closet that you never wear, others you wear all the time)
• **Style** (leading "like that"might be fine for someone else, not for you)
• **Routine** (your car could almost drive you to work by itself, right?)

Now, if what's inside is the comfort zone, then what's everything else outside it? Put another way, if you're standing inside the comfort zone, considering something outside of it, what does that zone out there look or *seem* like?

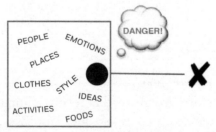

That little X outside the box is something that you've never done, but are considering. Let's say it's speaking in front of a huge audience. Or wake-boarding for the first time. Or having an emotional 1:1 conversation with someone in which you'll might show some vulnerability. Depending on you, one of those might be much further outside your comfort zone than the others.

Either way, as you're standing literally on the edge with one foot firmly planted inside and one foot on the edge, about to take a step out, we go back to that moment you relived at the beginning of this chapter. Your little voice is convinced that it's the danger zone out there, and will warn you louder and louder as you get close to that edge. We already know that your little voice steers you through most decisions, and it's either working for you, against you or in some other direction completely. It looks out into the unknown from inside your comfort zone, and says, *"You're not going to do that. That is the danger zone! You could fail. You could get rejected. Worst of all, you're going to look really bad!"*
Your little voice is very vested in you looking good all the time. Stepping out into that danger zone, you could definitely look pretty bad, even stupid. So we usually don't. Unless we do.

Getting Out

Gotta Go.
For as may times as your little voice has encouraged you to go further than you thought you could, it's also held you back from opportunities that have presented themselves along your path, right? Notice the size of that box in relation to the rest of the page (representing the rest of the world in somebody's life). It's pretty small. And anything that gets too comfortable for too long starts to feel...

Boring and Small
We have all kinds of nice, polite ways to say this: "I'm burnt out, in a rut...stagnating...needing a change of scenery...having a midlife crisis...."

As people work more and more, and the division between our lives and our work blurs, we can get so busy we don't even realize that we've become fundamentally bored. We seem to just arrive there one day, right where we seemed just fine before. This is when we hear "I need a change" and see things like guys in their late 40s buying

motorcycles or extreme sports cars for the first time in their lives.
It's classic can't-stand-being-inside-comfort-zone-anymore-and-
need-to-get-out behavior.

Life Happens

Maybe it wasn't intentional—somebody (or life) decided for you. You
became a first-time parent. Bam-a little life is now dependent on you
every moment for the next 18 years. Or you were doing great at work,
and got promoted. Bam—now you have to lead instead of just produce.
Suddenly the playing field has changed, and you're back to Conscious-
Incompetent, outside your Comfort Zone.

Through Is the Only Way

There are some things we know we need to go through (or bust
through) in order to get to where we want to be. "Objects in mirror
are closer than they appear"is etched onto car rear-view mirrors. That
applies to our own psyche, too. Maybe it's a hard conversation you
know you need to have with someone, but have been avoiding. It seems
daunting, yet you know that nothing will change until you just do it.
It gnaws at you. Leading up to the actual breakthrough can be long
and painful. It either becomes a barrier to your advancement (in the
relationship, in your own thoughts), or you bite the bullet and take the
step. Often it ends up much easier and faster than you built it up to be
(hence the mirror).

That Leader You'd Like To Be

When we look at the leaders who get the most out of people and rise
way above everybody else's accomplishments, they're ones who are
able to have uninhibited impact...undaunted. They see possibility and
opportunity everywhere, not limited to just what they've done before
or see as safe. Leaders we see "pushing the envelope"in their impact
and work tend to also challenge their own comfort zones consistently.
I've rarely seen a legendary leader with huge impact who didn't have
an intentional regular practice of pushing themselves out of their
comfort zone. The bigger you can push your comfort zone, the bigger
your impact.

Taking the Step
Now let's go back to standing on the edge for a second. What happens
for you as you're standing on the edge, about to take the step? Some
people get butterflies in their stomach. Or a headache. Some get
sweaty. Or excited. Some get their heart racing really fast. Some start
talking really fast or making jokes or laughing. Some get silent. Or their
voice changes.
All of these things start to[1] happen as people get up to that edge.
*Think about what those signs are for you, and watch for them in your
people.*

What Drives You Out
Okay. So, there you are. You're feeling it. Either you're about to take
the step or you're not; you'll stay limited by your box or bust out. What
pushes you over the edge? Everybody has a different thing that gets
them to take the step. Could be...
• Encouragement and reassurance from others to go for it
• A cause to rally for
• A partner to do it with them
• A direct challenge — something/someone to prove wrong
• Someone else to go first
• Listing all that could be gained in a personal cost-benefit analysis
• Desperation (can't take it anymore)
• Inspiration
Take a minute to reflect on which of those fits for you most of the time.
This is key self-awareness so you can set yourself[2] up accordingly and
let your team know what to watch for and how they can support you.

As a leader, once you know what your key players need to take that step
and get past their voice, you can show up with the right trigger, just in
time.
For example, people in my world only need to tell me "There's no way
you can do that," and I instantly go for it. What do each of your key
partners need to take the step?

Doing It
Real life CZ Moment: I used to live in Chicago very close to the lake,

where there's an epic bike path full of people riding their bikes, going for runs, and rollerblading (yes, that's still a thing) all the time. I ran and rode my bike a lot, yet watched those bladers every day zooming past me so fast and doing tricks. I decided I was going to learn how to do it. It was outside my comfort zone, so I decided, "I know my little voice will take over if I let it, so I'll *purchase* the rollerblades—that way I'm financially invested and I have to do it," So, I get the rollerblades. I get all the gear on. I'm about to step out the door and my voice is screaming in my head, "What are you thinking? You have no idea what you're doing. You look ridiculous. You're going to fail at this and it's going to be bad," I did it anyway.

Reality Can Surprise You
Sometimes we get to the other side of that seemingly insurmountable CZ wall, and it goes better than we predicted. The act or conversation took minutes. The thing that had been draining your will and focus is then gone, and there's a proud mix of adrenaline, relief and newfound energy afterward. We breathe that sigh of relief, and instantly realize, "That wasn't as bad as I thought it would be."All of that worrying and prep, and we broke through it in moments. Like the rear-view mirror warning, some obstacles are smaller than they appear.

Reality Can Bite
Or sometimes we flail. So how did rollerblading go for me? Horribly. Really bad. The whole time I had an out-loud conversation with my little voice, saying things like, "I can do this. I can do this. Come on. Just stay with it," people looking at me like I was completely crazy, which I felt. And just as the little voice warned, I was a wreck, literally. I was teetering and falling, getting in people's way, even caused a bike collision. Actual rollerbladers yelled, "Get off the trail!"Finally—scraped, bruised, completely humiliated—it ended. This is reality. Remember trying to drive a stickshift that first time, going from blissfully ignorant to painfully conscious of how incompetent you were? A version of this often happens the first time we step outside the comfort zone. Instant success with a new thing you're learning? Probably not. While it's poetic when that happens, it's rare.

The Turtle Effect

If a turtle is out exploring, looking around, and it gets poked it in the face with a stick, it'll pull all the way into its shell and stay there—for a while. It would rather stay safe, in its shell as long as it needs to, than take that chance of making itself vulnerable again. We do this too...it goes horribly outside the CZ, so we recoil back into the box, further in than where we started, safe. "Okay, little voice, you were right." So my rollerblades went back into the closet, where they stayed for quite a long time.

Then it's Decision Time.

What happens next is what separates people who play big or end up playing consistently smaller than they could.

Remember fixed and growth mindset[3] from Carol Dweck's research? She writes, "People in a growth mindset don't just seek challenge, they thrive on it. The bigger the challenge, the more they stretch." They feel smart when they figure out and conquer something that was challenging at first. People in a fixed mindset sell their metaphorical rollerblades.

They need it to go well right away, because to them immediate success at something defines their capability.

You also remember Martin Seligman's research about optimism and pessimism, yes?[4] Someone's *explanatory style*[5] has a lot to do with how they stick with it or give up when stepping out of that comfort zone.

Every time I passed that closet on my way out for a safe run, those rollerblades taunted me from the back of the closet, "Wimp, wimp, wimp, I knew you couldn't do it,"until I couldn't take it anymore. I had something to prove to myself. So, I got the rollerblades back out, and made myself do it anyway until, many fails later, I was actually rollerblading. It wasn't pretty, but I was doing it.

We make our way (remember your process from Chapter #3) through that uncomfortable learning phase to consciously competent.

It took me a whole summer to be able to rollerblade *and* have headphones on *and* not be in fear of a dog or other human causing me to have to stop or turn.

Comfort Zone Expands
At a certain point the comfort zone bumps out to include what was once distinctly outside. This occurs immediately if it was just an objects-in-the-mirror-appear-closer-than-they-are, one-time issue. It happens over time and practice if we're learning something new. Bigger comfort zone = Fewer limiters = Bigger influence.

The Growth Zone
So...now that we look at it...is it really the danger zone outside that CZ?

Nah—that's little voice language. It's more accurately labeled *growth zone*. Anytime you deliberately take a step out of your comfort zone, you're there.

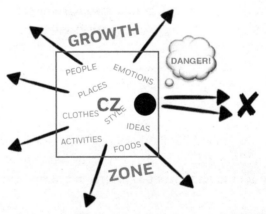

Leading It
And if you think about it as a leader, what are you asking people to do every single day? Every time you introduce some new request, challenge, skill to learn, area to master, area to handle... you're asking them to step outside their comfort zone. Hmm.

We know that people trust and follow what you *do* over what you *say*, so as you ask them to keep continually stepping out of their CZs, how are they seeing you do the same? If you're not, you become a hypocrite to them. To have a team of people who are stepping outside their comfort zones, taking on new challenges and expanding into the growth zone, then you need to *Be the model*, stepping out visibly and audibly.

This gets tricky as your leadership position gets more prominent. The stakes of your decisions get higher, the value of your expertise and mastery more focused. You spent a lot (time, work, rungs) earning that credibility, so the tendency is to do whatever you can to stay solidly in that expertise. That's very different from you in the *growth zone*, which is squishy. Stepping out feels vulnerable. So, you might stretch your CZ, but only on your own time, when nobody can see, so they don't have to see you flail. Except if your people never see you stepping out, they never get the model or see you as human, and don't feel permission to do it themselves. This is where we see teams who are afraid to step out, playing safe and small all the time, not wanting to fail or show a mistake.

Counter-Intuition

One of my favorite researchers is Dr. Brene Brown, a vulnerability expert. Her first TED talk went viral within 24 hours because she hit a nerve we all have...that there's a conflict in how we view vulnerability in ourselves vs. how we view it in other people. Think about a leader who stands up and shares something personal, who admits a mistake, who visibly takes a step out there and then carries on, strong. Universally, we're inspired by that, yet we don't want to do it ourselves. As Brown points out, we tend to see vulnerability as "courage in you, but weakness in me." A dilemma, right? Brown asserts that "Vulnerability may actually be our most accurate measure of courage. In 15,000 pieces of data, I could not find one instance of courage that wasn't completely underpinned by vulnerability."[6]

So, with that, think for a moment about your own comfort zone, and how you protect it in the name of credibility and strength. How could you step out, showing some human vulnerability, to blaze the trail for your team to step out?

It's time.

What have you been avoiding, working around or wishing you could do? Where do you know you need to push yourself into the growth zone? Where are you playing small? If you're feeling a little bit of that discomfort thinking about it, you're on the right track. So, it just depends on you, where your little voice pops up, and paying attention to those nuances.

How to expand your zone...

Mark your territory.

What are some things that you know you already do well or comfortably as a leader? This list can be as comprehensive as you want it to be. If you want to write a volume on this subject, that's totally fine. It's important to get clear about what's already inside your comfort zone. Next, call out where could you need to step out. Think about some of the things we've explored so far. *Own your strengths so you build from there.* At the end of this chapter, take a few minutes to map out your strengths, and how you can build out.

Look around.

A great way to identify areas to stretch outside your comfort zone is to look at other leaders and the moves they make which you don't. Or recall situations in which you've thought, "Ugh, I wish I could do that," or "This is not a strong area for me," or even "Not my style." All big red flags. *Then pick one. Or a few.*

Step out enough.

Make sure you're actually stretching yourself to step out in a way that will challenge and stretch your ability to play life bigger, influence further, thrive more solidly. So, while putting my clothes away more often might be different from my norm, it's not a comfort zone issue. I avoid putting my clothes away because I just don't like to do it — *not* because it's a stretch for me. I need to pick a true stretch.

On the flip side, if you have a fear of heights and want to break through it, I don't recommend skydiving as a first step. That's too far. Climbing a ladder with a spotter behind you would be a better start—bigger than standing on top of a chair, but not quite skydiving. *Pick something that will stretch you, not disable you.*

So is bigger always better? Not necessarily. This isn't about jumping into the unknown everywhere with reckless abandon—that's volatile leadership, which you don't want. Great leaders are strategic and focused, but not limited by their boundaries, which takes a delicate balance of agility. Holding that tension between strength and stepping out takes self-awareness, willingness to call oneself out, and ability to learn efficiently and voraciously. Did I end up a trick-rollerblader? No. But I did learn a lot about my abilities, stretched my capacity, and even got some critical balance things worked out, which helped me have the confidence to successfully step out of my comfort zone another way — surfing (which went much better than blading the first time). This is what learners do—keep stretching bigger, so strengths build other strengths, undaunted.

Map it.
Write down what the benefit of doing this is for you—what's your WIIFM? What will you have? What confidence might you have that you don't have now? What would you be able to take on that you can't now? Then identify what it will take for you to do it—who you'll need to *be* (brave? confident? strong? grounded? human?). What support will you need to be that? Sounding familiar? *Set yourself up.*

Push it.
Keep the rollerblading example in mind. Don't just do it one time. Do it as many times as you need to, making sure to tweak and refine each time, until you can say, "I can do this," and can add it to your repertoire. The number one way people keep themselves from a bigger game is quitting too soon. It doesn't work immediately and/or looks silly, so we do it a couple more times, and they say, "Yeah—that's enough." But maybe it was really too soon to tell. *Keep going.*

Record it.

The next time you get up against your CZ wall, your voice will start all over again, and you'll want some ammo. So as you bust through now, capture the process for yourself (notes, voicemail you leave for yourself, artifact from the experience) so you can remind yourself of why it's worth it the next time around. *What did your little voice say? What did you do to overcome that? What happened after you stepped out and got more comfortable? How did that little voice calm down or quiet down? What was your reaction? What were other people's reactions?*

The bigger your comfort zone, the bigger your opportunity for uninhibited impact. That's what we want for you—no situation that you come upon where you say, "I don't think so" because it's new territory. You're playing big and taking it on, as influencers do.

So, go ahead and step out. Have fun. Kick your own butt. Challenge your borders. Get into the growth zone.
Play Bigger.

Then take your people there, too.

Notes:

"State is highly contagious. One person gets sour, and it starts to spread... and the person with the strongest State wins."

Chapter 9: State

What if you could get yourself from bored to fired up on demand?
What if you could call out grouchiness on your team, and have it change it instantly?
What if you could access the same kind of focus as professional athletes do?

While most can't, you can. And actually *choose* how your moments, interactions and days go rather than just allowing them to happen to you.

It's all about **State**, and you're in one right now. Not geographic state like California, but State defined as *where you are mentally, emotionally and physically at any given moment.* You could be any of the following right now...

Productive States	Unproductive States
curious	tired
excited	irritated
calm	bored
focused	grouchy
creative	cynical
intrigued	angry
reflective	distracted
motivated	anxious
open	defensive
	stressed
	complacent

Often people refer to their mood, which refers mostly to emotion. Yet there's a lot more to where you are right now than emotion, and you can change it more easily than you'd think. This is one of my favorite topics to coach, because you can get huge shifts and see the impact very quickly. It's also a differentiator we see in masters; think Michael Jordan, Jackie Joyner, Tiger Woods, each in their prime. Not only are they legendary masters of their talent, they were also masters of their own State from second to second; under tremendous pressure, they could get and hold themselves perfectly aligned mentally, emotionally AND physically to outperform everyone else. This is key not just for athletes, but also for you and those you're leading, too. Because...

Performance is State-dependent.
Learning is State-dependent.
Attention is State-dependent.
Focus is State-dependent.

In other words, *Whether or not a person **can** perform, learn* or focus as you want or need to completely depends on his/her State.

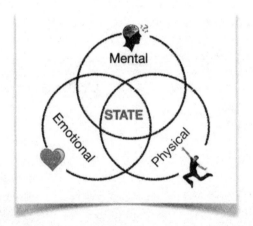

State always comprises its three interconnected parts. Change one part, and you change them all.
Every time.

Think about it...

You're working, start to lose focus, so get up and walk around for a minute. You sit back down, and you're refocused.
You changed physical -> it shifted you mentally and emotionally.

You're tired, but talk yourself into working out anyhow. You don't even get winded, have energy that surprises you, and get into a great workout.
That's mental —> shifting where you were physically and emotionally.

You're feeling cranky and sluggish, then someone calls or texts who always makes your day. You come away from your phone happy, energized, thinking more clearly.
That's emotional —> changing where you were emotionally/mentally.

Those are all called State Changes, and you actually have lots of them all day long.

Happening Or Choosing

States get triggered by all sorts of things...situations, conversations, episodes. Recurring triggers exist all over — called *anchors*, or associations to particular States. Common anchors are:

- *Certain people*... just seeing their name come up on your voicemail list triggers a certain State
- *Smells*... a sniff of a certain cologne/perfume can instantly take you back to a certain person in your memory.
- *Music*... that's why your favorite show doesn't change its theme song — it's your trigger for an excited, anticipatory State to be ready for tuning in.
- *Places*... that one spot where you will always trigger the same memory and State you were in.

The mind-body connection has lots of research, and we've even come to reference "mind over matter" to explain how we perform despite ourselves or as a tactic to employ when we need to get "in the zone." That's really State we're referencing, in moments when we've deliberately taken control of it — changed, accessed, set it so well that we could perform beyond the circumstances or what we normally would. Athletes and entertainers do this[1] all the time pregame or pre-show, in order to set themselves for their best performance. Why not you?

Mastering It

Master your State, and you guarantee your own performance. The easiest State examples to watch are in sports. It's a great fishbowl where we can study moments, patterns and techniques of State mastery or examples of State fails — all as spectators.

Take basketball... The foul shot in basketball is the ultimate test of State. Technically, it's the easiest shot there is — a straight set shot, nobody interfering, the same every time. And yet... elite, uber-talented professional basketball players screw up this shot. Some chronically. Why?

Because it's also the hardest shot in basketball, as a pure on-display test of being able to set and hold State. There's no question of whether a pro player can physically make that shot — of course they can; they have and will nail thousands of foul shots, maybe even with their eyes closed. Yet they get to the foul line with pressure of the win in jeopardy, and it's not about physical or technical ability anymore. If mental and/or emotional aren't locked in, it literally handicaps their physical ability in that moment, and they can't physically make the shot.

Change one, you change them all. All connected, all the time.

So, you may not be playing professional basketball right now, but it's similar. It's not always about whether you have the brilliance, but how consistently can you *access it* when you need it. And your performance likely has more at stake than that player on the foul line. Yours is about performing as the right leader to unlock what's possible on your team, create the groundbreaking idea, or listen to another human being in a way that causes them to step into their awesomeness or completely shut down. Your State critically matters.

You may have an important strategy session to lead, where your mental agility and focus are critical for a huge initiative you're leading. Yet if something's off for you emotionally, you literally cannot focus, right? Just like that pro can't make the foul shot.

Or, maybe you're normally great at being emotionally present. Your significant other is having a meltdown about something, and really needs you to just listen and be there for them. But you're completely mentally consumed with a deadline you're about to miss for work. You try to listen to your partner, but cannot get present. *Mental* is hijacking your *emotional*, right? Another missed shot.

Think of it as the glue that holds everything else (your talent, your ability, your knowledge) to-gether. If you have those things and you can master your State, you're set. If you have all that, but can't hold your State, you're inconsistent at best.

So let's get you some State mastery, yes?

Wake up a new self-awareness... of your State.

First, you have to be able to call it in the moment. What State are you in right now? (Hopefully it's something like curious, focused, or intrigued as you're reading this.) "Good" and "bad" don't cut it for pinpointing a State. Start calling it specifically, like something on that list at the beginning of the chapter. If you find yourself thinking "I don't know what State I'm in," it's just because this is a new lens you're seeing yourself through—it'll get clearer.

Pay close attention to WHAT, WHO and WHEN triggers your State.

You'll notice that you might be in a really great State...but then it gets messed with, spinning you into an unproductive State. Or the opposite —you're in blah State and something can shift it immediately to fire you up into an awesome State. It can change in an instant from any number of mental, emotional or physical triggers around you, some in the direction you want to go, others not. Pay attention.

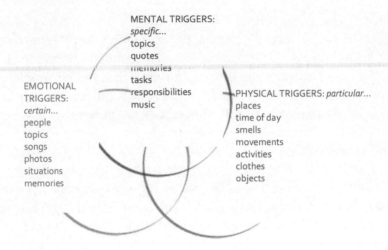

MENTAL TRIGGERS:
specific...
topics
quotes
memories
tasks
responsibilities
music

EMOTIONAL
TRIGGERS:
certain...
people
topics
songs
photos
situations
memories

PHYSICAL TRIGGERS: *particular...*
places
time of day
smells
movements
activities
clothes
objects

Here's why this is key...

State affects everything.

I mentioned earlier that attention, learning and performance are completely State-dependent. In other words, the performance you're able to bring completely depends on the State you're in. Think about a recent great day, great presentation, great meeting, great conversation. Now think about the State you were in at the time. It was probably focused, energized, into it, engaged...something on your "top 5 productive States"list, right? How would that have gone if you were in an unproductive State like tired, irritated, or distracted. Way different, right?

State is highly contagious. Always. And it's happening on your team a lot. One person gets sour, and it starts to spread[2], right? In a leadership position or close partnership, this is even more magnified for you than for anybody else; your State is determining other people's State the second you walk in the door. They check yours out immediately, and theirs changes to either match, deal with or avoid yours. We've all noticed this before. The boss (or partner, or family member) walks in and is in some kind of a grouchy, snappy, salty State. Or walks in in a fun, energized state. Everyone's state gets affected by that, right? We all fall victim to one another's State, and the person with the strongest (or most negative) State wins, as it spreads to others.

Negative State is unfortunately more powerful than positive. If just one person is in a negative state on a team with three people in positive states, that negative can contaminate and take down the others quickly.

Dr. Barbara Fredrickson[3] has shown both in practical and lab research that within someone's own outlook, one negative emotion has to be outnumbered by three positive emotions in order for people to thrive.

When you spot a negative State, call it or change it immediately, before it spreads.

Accidentally contaminate or Intentionally elevate.
Because you can (and do) contaminate somebody else's creative blissful State with your irritat-ed, pessimistic one or elevate somebody in a depressed, isolated State to engaged, inspired and connected without even trying,you've got to make sure your State is in a good place before you walk in the door. Your State getting all over folks is like toothpaste out of the tube—you can't undo it. Your snippy interactions with people in a temporarily negative State will send ripples of reaction through your team and people's psyche long after you've moved on to a great State an hour later (you still remember that one nasty blowup with someone three years ago and fear its reccurance, right?). It takes ridiculously more time and energy to get them back to a great State as it does to just get yours right to begin with.

Your State
Here's the difference between the masses and those people who go beyond to influence, lead with impact and outperform...

Choose it.
Most people are victims of their own State. It's 10 a.m. and they've already given up, saying, "Yeah, it's just going to be one of those days." Wow.
Stuff happens around us all of the time that messes with us mentally, emotionally and physically. The question is...how are you going to respond to it in a way that keeps you solid? Maybe you only had a few

hours of sleep last night or are coming from a particularly tough conversation just now. So what? Don't let that determine your State or set it for the day. Choose it. People are watching you.

To choose and change/set your State, pick one of the three ways into it, or several to make it more potent. Depending on how strong your current State is (like the one you're trying to change out of) some methods will work faster/easier than others.

Deliberately change it.
The State changes that will become your go-to's are the ones you anchor solidly and tweak to perfection. Take what I've given you here, add on to it, then get your complete list onto your phone, your wall or somewhere you can see and access it easily because the moments you really need a State change are the ones, in which you can't think of one to save your life. When in doubt, remember—physical is the fastest to manipulate easily; despite the war you may be having with yourself in your head (mental, emotional), you can force yourself to do something physical pretty quickly. Move your body, and your State will follow.

State Changes:
- Think about a time when you were totally successful
- Listen to specific music (relaxing music to calm down, upbeat music to get energy, favorite song to get psyched...
- Have someone tell you a joke
- Look at a picture of a favorite person
- Read an inspirational quote
- Go for a walk or quick jog around the building
- Splash cold water on your face
- Re-read a great note, card or email someone gave you which put you in a great State
- Drink lots of water (gets more fluid in system, brain operates more clearly)
- High-5 someone
- Look at something in nature (like a cloud passing in the sky) for a few solid minutes.
- Drink caffeine

- Ask someone in your immediate space to tell you their favorite thing about one of their friends/kids/you
- Stand up and stretch
- Recall a time you felt completely loved and accepted by someone
- Do some jumping jacks
- Get something to eat with extra protein, light on the starches.
- Visualize yourself nailing whatever then next challenge is- all the way through to the celebration at the end.

Get strategic.
You now have a new awareness, and soon you'll also have a new muscle of *State Control* to flex in response to your world, moment to moment. Yet the power of State in your performance, influence and accomplishment will come in how you use State strategically. Steven Covey[4] taught us to "start with the end in mind" and that everything's created twice— first in your head, then a second time in real life. Most interpret this as planning without ever considering *Be* or *State* in the plan.. a huge miss. This sounds like Be-Do-Have because it's part of it—BE is the big header, State is the nuance. To *be Visionary*, I might first need to get into a focused, open, creative State. We can watch two leaders execute identical plans, and get wildly different results. Often it comes down to which leader can hold their own State or change other people's State intentionally to determine performance, focus and contagious attention despite what's being thrown at them.

Remember Chapter #4? Venus Williams would never step onto the court without getting her State locked in first. So why would you do so on the court of your life? Those superstars intentionally choose their State rather than letting their State control them. Get deliberate.

Favorite song that fires you up?
Listen to it before the big presentation.
Place that stresses you?
Get out of there and avoid it when it counts.
Shirt that makes you feel invincible?
Wear it for the big meeting.

Scent that calms you?
Wear it when you know you're anxious.
Photo that reminds you of a great/successful/peaceful/
connected moment?
*Get it onto your wall or phone where you can look at it
when you need it.*

Map *state changes* strategically into your plan for ideating with the
team, working with that one person who pushes your buttons, cranking
out all the content, heads-down, pitching to your potentials,
facilitating the stakeholders, going into that one week you know will
test you, calling out and celebrating the wins of the team (even when
you'd like them to be further along).
Every one of these will need you to be in a different State to guarantee
its ease and success. Choose them proactively and intentionally.

And then there's everyone else's State. You can directly change that,
too.

Their State

*"Excuse me, but can you get your foul State off of me, please? I'm trying
to be creative and in-spired here, and you're contaminating it with your
irritated grouchiness, which is getting all over everyone. Please go
handle that."*

What would it be like to work on a team where you could actually say
that to someone? I'm here to testify that it's actually possible, and can
be awesome. Maybe you won't start off quite that pointed, but I can get
you close.

Once you've got a handle on your own State (which you'll tinker with
for a lifetime), you're halfway there, since your State is the model for
theirs, and they're watching you all the time. So now it's time to
directly take on something just as clutch... other people's States. As
we've established, most people have little awareness of their own State
and even less aptitude in effectively changing it. So until they do (and
even after), it'll be YOU in many moments who will need to do it *for*

them.

Check them out.
As a leader, start paying attention as much to your people's State as those other things you monitor, like what they're contributing, focusing on and doing. It's fueling all of those things already, so addressing those without State is like treating the symptoms instead of curing the issue causing them. This gets you to the core of what makes them awesome (or not) moment to moment. Your ability to facilitate their State is directly proportional to their motivation, focus and productivity.

So—two key questions:
1. **What State are they in?** and...
2. **Is it the best State for them to be in** (for the task at hand, the news you're about to drop on them, the next XX hours you're about to spend with them, the way their State is spreading to others etc.)?

Cues tell all.
Most of our communication is nonverbal. What we feel and think manifests itself in our tonality, body language, eye movements, breathing and facial expression. It's incredibly hard to fake these things, and the people you're with tell you a lot about where they are without ever uttering a word. While we could spend the rest of this book on how to study and interpret[5] and respond to those micro-changes, the biggest thing to start noticing with people is their non-verbal patterns. You might observe that a colleague has particular facial expressions and body language that show up consistently when they're nervous, even if they say they're "fine." Practice first paying attention to the cues, then labeling them in your mind as different States (excited, bored, curious, sad, irritated, reflective, pumped up, grouchy, inspired...). Then, watch people in their moments with you, and ask yourself if the State they're in is a good one for what's happening, or not.

If not, then get busy...

Change it from the outside in.
You can change someone else's State in a second. In fact you might do it all the time... Someone is *resistant*, for instance. While just before this meeting you observed them talking to someone else with lots of varied tonality, quite animated, open postured, bright-eyed and smiling. They sit down with you, and there's a visible shift—their jaw becomes set, their brow slightly furrowed, their voice becomes monotone and forced. Yet ask a simple question that gets them to think about something else completely (a topic you know they love). That person's now in a more *open* and *receptive* state before you begin.

Or... you and a teammate are brainstorming on a question with you recording at the whiteboard. At one point you switch spots—you hand over the marker to your partner to get him up and writing as you then walk around the room, and suddenly new ideas are flowing for you both.

Or... you are presenting to a group, and see their eyes glazing over, as *bored* State starts to take over the room. You have everyone quickly stand up, you pose a question for them all to answer out loud, then have them sit back down. Now they're *awake* and *engaged*.

Some outside-in State-changes are deliberate breaks in pattern, others quick energy resets:

Switch it Up — Early and often.
Those State changes are key when someone's in an overtly negative or low-energy state, as each will break the pattern they're in, changing their State to something more engaged, positive or higher energy. The higher the energy, the better in most cases.

That said, your team needs deliberate State Changes more than you think. The average attention span correlates with age (like five minutes max for a five year old)...up to about age 18, at which point it maxes out. So 20 minutes is about the limit of most people's attention span (outside of gaming and other immersive altered-state activities). All attempts of "plowing through" beyond that window are a waste of time and energy, because once State is gone, so is focus, learning and performance. Instead, change State! All you and your team need is a reset of attention — a State Change — about every 20 minutes in your work process, and the brain/performance/focus stays fresh.

Try These:
• Have them tell you about their last success with this team in vivid detail. (mental)
• Take them for a walk. (physical)
• Change the subject completely. (mental)
• Continue the conversation standing up if you were sitting. (physical)
• Give them a compliment. (emotional)
• Give them a high-five. (physical)
• Tell them a joke. (emotional)
• Everyone rotate positions in the room. (physical)
• Ask their opinion about something you know they care about. (mental/emotional)
• Toss them a ball. (physical)
• Offer them a snack or drink, like a bottle of water or a cup of coffee. (physical)
• Change or put on some music with the energy you're going for. (mental/physical/emotional)
• Show them a hilarious or inspiring or thoughtful or intriguing post or video online. (emotional)

Call it. Once you and your team understand State, you can then own it and call it with one another. I've witnessed productivity and morale of high-stakes teams be transformed with it. On those teams, everyone is responsible for his/her own State, making sure it's productive, conducive to what the team's up to, and able to help others accelerate. They incorporate State Changes as regular team practice into their work, which makes all the difference. You'll see high-fiving between agenda topics, movement as they work, koosh balls flying purposefully to engage the right States, and people owning their own attention, performance and focus with their State.

And when they don't, someone calls it.

And then you'll hear...

"Actually, you're absolutely right. My grouchy State isn't helping anyone — I apologize for getting it on you. I need a State Change. I'll be back in a few minutes, better."

And then they go, take a few minutes to change their State, re-engage, and the team's on its way. It's a beautiful thing, and you can have that on your team.

Take it on!

Notes:

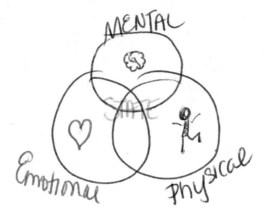

MENTAL

EMOTIONAL

PHYSICAL

Learning
Performance
Attention

} State
Dependant

"Almost anyone you work with has all three of these modalities at their disposal at any moment. They are tapping into Visual, Auditory and Kinesthetic no matter what their diagnostics say... all the time, every day."

Chapter 10:
VAK

Do you talk to yourself (out loud) often?
Can you picture what you wore at your last few important presentations?
Is your workspace set up for comfort? If not, do you wish it were?

Whether or not you answered "yes" or "no" to those three questions has everything to do with your wiring. Before I explain, let's first find out what yours is.

On *www.sarahsingerandco.com* is a quick and free Modality Indicator in the diagnostics section of the site. Take a few moments now to go complete that, and then come back, and we'll decode it.

Welcome back!

So when you're trying to communicate with someone and it seems like you're speaking two completely different languages, it's because you sort of are. Or when you're relating to another person's communication quickly and easily? Maybe it's because they're matching you.

Modalities Matter
One of the biggest a-ha realizations in my life was as a teenager, when I realized that I naturally thought, communicated and learned differently from how I was being taught[1] most of the time. Learning how to translate what other people were doing/saying radically opened up my ability to understand, connect and communicate. This mismatch could be happening between you and those folks you'd like to influence.

What we now know about which pathways in the brain are being used at any given moment is astounding, thanks to neuroscientists and brain research. That's growing so fast, it's hard to keep up with, but here's one thing we do know—there are lots of different paths that communication and ideas can travel in our thinking, and we have preferences. In the diagnostic you just took, you probably found that one of those modalities came out as more dominant than the others. So you can really see, hear and grasp these three modalities, try this little experiment...

First, put your hands over your eyes like you're blocking the sun, making a visor for your eyes. With your hands in that position, look up as you say (out loud) the word "**Visual**."
Do that really quickly right now.

Next, take your hands and cup them around your ears like you're trying to hear something better. With your hands there, say the word "**Auditory**." *Do that really quickly right now. Tell your little voice to relax—it's okay. Nobody can see you.*

Finally, take your hands and kind of brush your legs twice (like you're trying to brush crumbs off), and then bring both hands to your heart, okay? That's three movements, as you say a three-syllable word— "**Kinesthetic**." *Do that really quickly right now. It's completely worth it, as you'll remember this moment and the learning that went with it vividly.*

Now, why did I have you do that just now? We did just talk about comfort zone, right? There's that, plus by doing those motions and saying the words as you did them, you just tapped and anchored those concepts with all three modalities. Now it's time to learn a little more about them, how they work and how you can make communication easier with them.

Visual is anything you can see, read, write or visualize in your head.

Auditory is anything you hear, say, think about saying or hear in your mind.

Kinesthetic (has two parts) is anything you do (brushing off your legs) and emotionally feel (hands on your heart).

You use all three modalities all the time, just like most everyone. You write and type and take notes[2], maybe even doodle or sketch. You listen and talk to people every day, exploring ideas and directions. You do and feel things all day.

Now What?

You're about to dive into understanding the three modalities with super-specificity. So what can you do with this information? Here's the thing... Almost[3] anyone you work with has all three of these modalities at their disposal at any moment. They are Stapping into visual, auditory and kinesthetic no matter what their diagnostics say all the time every day. So...

• Start noticing, listening for and catching on to people's preferences.
• Enter the modality of the person you're working with 1:1, and everything shifts. You'll have their attention, their rapport, and their partnership.
• Incorporate all three modalities into your delivery, and instantly you're speaking everyone's language instead of just relating to those with the same preference as you.

Debate Alert!

There's a lot of critique on the "validity" of VAK as learning styles, so let's clear this up now. Some academics have attempted to officially debunk it as an irrelevant theory based on some clinical trials they've run. Yet their tests have been limited in some important ways, their conclusions inaccurate and in gross conflict with my observations of hundreds of thousands of learners and educators over several decades. They tested the idea of whether teaching someone through their preferred modality makes it easier for them to learn something or not. Except they didn't use neutral content in the studies. Their tests show things like teaching a geography lesson to an auditory learner *only through auditory means* (strictly talking them through it, not showing it to them), which didn't work.

Of course it didn't, because despite someone's modality preference Geography is *visual content*; so for anyone to learn it they have to see the countries on the map in spatial relation to one another!

My conclusions and recommendations are based on a myriad of content, taught through all three modalities, to see if any are easier than the others for learners. I've watched understanding and learning become easy for so many people when it had been such a struggle before- with just a modality change. I've studied how people best create ideas in the first place (ie: left to their own preferences, which way do they go?), and modality matters critically there. Since we have yet to see *neutral* clinical studies, let's go with my 10,000+ hours of observation and coaching in this arena.

Visual
Don't imagine a green elephant with purple polka dots right now.

You just pictured it, didn't you? Because I just tapped into your visual modality. You use this mode countless times throughout the course of the day. Your eyes visually take in the world around you as you find your way and process information in that language through texts, emails, and so on. As you're formulating something to say, you might create a picture in your mind. As you're planning something out, you might see it happen in your mind first.

You definitely have visual thinkers to influence. Here's what you need to understand about how they think...

Visual thinkers think in pictures and mental movies. It's as if they are camera-heads and they're recording snapshots or video of everything that's happening to them all the time. They remember things by replaying those images. For example, I could map out right now for you each of the complete scenes as each of my three kids were born 15, 12 and 10 years ago—the room interiors, exactly how the light was shining, where everyone was standing in the room, what people were wearing and the looks on their faces during key moments. I could replay each with pretty great accuracy, as most visual people could for important moments in their life.

"I See What You're Saying."
Language is a great tip-off to somebody's modality preference. Visual people use visual words...

"**Picture** this."
"I **see** what you're saying."
"**Look!**" (if they want to get your attention)
"Ah, that's **crystal clear**."
"I just want to **watch and see** how this plays out."
"I really need you to **paint a picture** for me of how this is going to look."
"Allow me to **illustrate** how this should go."
"I just need a little **preview** of what's going to happen in this meeting."
"We really need to **expose** all the issues here."
"We really need to **clarify** what's the most important thing."
"I don't know. I think his judgment is a little **cloudy** right now."
"Well, I don't know, that's really **foggy** to me."

If they're really listening carefully, a visual person's head and body might be pretty still, although while they're speaking they might move quickly with lots of hand gestures and big movements, like they're painting a picture with their hands. They speak quickly, because that video is playing out in their head faster than they can talk, and they're trying to keep up. If they can use visual aids or talk with you near a whiteboard where they can show you what they mean, everything gets clearer.

See it to Believe it

Visual people pay attention to, trust and remember *what they see*. To them, if it's important then you will write it somewhere obvious or email it, so do that. If it's an important deadline, it'll be posted, so do that. If there's a plan, get it mapped out.

So, let's just say that you're leading a meeting and you've got some visual folks in the meeting. You write some things up on the white board. They will keep coming back to what you wrote, reading those as the most important things to focus on because they're up there. If you have an equally important point that you don't write down, a visual person will miss it because, to them, if it were important, of course you would've written it!

The visual thinker needs a physical or mental image to go with your point. If you can give a graph, add color, sketch what you mean, they'll stay with you longer and think with you faster. If you're not so visual, have them do it. Have them come up with a depiction of it while you're talking or be the scribe who gets it all up on the whiteboard. They'll probably be able to do it more accurately than you will.

They also need to have an overall view and purpose. It's very important to them to get a clear picture of where you're going with something from the beginning.

All in the Eyes

As you're talking to a visual person, check for alignment with them by watching their eyes. If they're right there with you, their eyes are wide open and they're looking straight at you or they're looking up to picture what you're saying. If they're confused, in disagreement, or not quite sure about what you're saying, their eyes will start to squint or shift around. They'll make faces (mostly around the eyes, eyebrows) to express how they feel about what you're saying, without even realizing it.

Details

Visual people will remember the last time you wore that outfit, and be completely distracted by the coffee spot on your sleeve from this morning. They will also point out your typos. Don't take it personally. They do this with themselves, too. They like things to be visually clean—their work beautiful, their surroundings organized, maybe even color-coded, everything in its place.

Visual people are also a little bit cautious until they're crystal clear mentally about something. If they can't get a picture in their head that's totally focused, they're not going to jump right into something. Imagine that their brain is like a manual 35-millimeter camera. Whatever it is that you're laying out for them, they have to get the picture lined up and composed in perfect focus before they actually snap the photo. If it's a little fuzzy for them (literally), they'll keep asking questions or holding back until they get it clear. Focus on clarity when it comes to the visual people you lead.

So, as we take a look at a visual person, or how great would it be, if you knew how to speak their language? If you knew how to process the cues that they're giving you, if you knew how to give them what they need, so that they could get it quickly and hold onto it?
The communication between you will accelerate. Try these in a 1:1 conversation or meeting...

1:1 with Vanessa Visual:

- Sit across a table from her, making sure she can look you square in the eyes.
- Choose a location where you won't be visually distracted.
- Before you begin, paint a picture for her of how the session will go.
- Physically show her your notes as you are giving them to her.
- Whiteboard as you go, so she see what you're doing and talking about.
- Show her the big picture first- highlights first, then details.
- Use a highlighter (or 2 colors for pro & con), and mark points as you cover them or highlight the main points.
- Welcome and encourage her to take notes as you go.
- Use phrases like "look", "I see", "it looks like", "I can picture you...","do you see what I'm saying?"
- Watch and check her eye expressions throughout- squinting = something's wrong or she disagrees.
- Create a list, chart, or graph of what you'll be talking about, do. Do an overview first, and then explain your points.
- Follow up with an email or text afterward, thanking her for the time. something's wrong or she disagrees.
- Create a list, chart, or graph of what you'll be talking about, do. Do an overview first, and then explain your points

Here's a quick cue card to reference for Visual folks you'd like to influence. Experiment with these, and notice that some people respond quickly to them (there are your Visuals!)

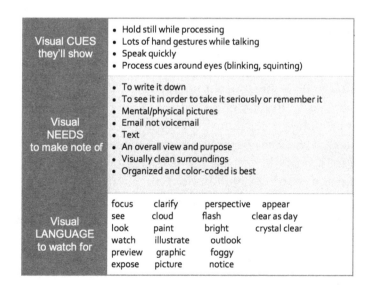

Visual CUES they'll show	• Hold still while processing • Lots of hand gestures while talking • Speak quickly • Process cues around eyes (blinking, squinting)			
Visual NEEDS to make note of	• To write it down • To see it in order to take it seriously or remember it • Mental/physical pictures • Email not voicemail • Text • An overall view and purpose • Visually clean surroundings • Organized and color-coded is best			
Visual LANGUAGE to watch for	focus see look watch preview expose	clarify cloud paint illustrate graphic picture	perspective flash bright outlook foggy notice	appear clear as day crystal clear

Auditory

Go ahead and sing "Happy Birthday" to yourself in your head right now. It's okay—we can't hear you.

Uh-oh. That might be stuck in a loop now—sorry. That's your Auditory modality. You use it all day as you talk with people, selectively listen to what's happening around you, cue up conversations in your head and replay what's been discussed, decided and stated.

You have two channels for it:
Auditory-In = everything you hear.
Auditory-Out = everything you say.

Clearly you use both a lot, yet which one engages your brain more? When you're listening, there's definitely a whole series of pathways being used, processing what you hear. But to *say it* out loud engages a lot more of your brain, which is a good thing. Plus we're all a legend in our own minds, so find more natural interest in what we say ourselves moreso than what someone else says, right? So anytime you can have people say it themselves instead of listening to you say it, they'll remember, engage and own it more

Of course you need to make it *ring* for the Auditory thinkers you want to influence. Here's what you hear from them...

They think in dialogue and soundtrack.
Just like the visual thinker had a camera in their head, an auditory person is an audio-recorder-head, recording Voice Memos of everything everyone says, creating new soundtracks all the time. They think through things best out loud, and love to talk. They love discussion and chatting about things. If they're working through a decision, they'll want to talk it through with somebody, posing different questions aloud. If nobody's there to do that with, they'll just talk to themselves, out loud. They record as they interact with you, then, when they want to recall something from that interaction, they go through the audio files in their head, pull out the one from that conversation, and replay it. If they tell you that you said it a certain way

five months ago, believe it—their recordings are pretty exact. Because their brains record in sequence, sequence is important for them. It's rough to interrupt an auditory person when they talk for that reason. It completely messes with their sequence of thought, and when you're done interrupting, instead of picking right back up where they left off, they'll go back to the beginning of whatever they said, and start again. Similarly, if you had a plan in a particular sequence, and then you mess with that sequence, it's going to mess with an auditory person. They have to go back and literally re-record it in the new sequence they'll need for reference. So, give them that time to do so.

"I Hear What You're Saying."
Often auditory communicators speak rhythmically, with some natural melody to their voice. They are sensitive to volume and tonality, and will pick up on the stress in your voice faster than other people will. Auditory thinkers use auditory language.

Listen for these...

"**Listen!**"
"You're not **listening** to me."
"You're not **hearing** me." "Oh, you are **hearing** me."
"Ah, I **hear** ya."
"**Sounds** like we got a plan."
"I don't like your **tone**."
"Umm, I **hear a note** of sarcasm in what you're saying."
"I think we really need to **broadcast** this particular part of the project."
"Ah, let's really make that idea **ring**."
"Oh, that really **clicks** for me."
"I just need to **talk** this through..."
"Let's just **ask** this question."

Say it's so.
While the Visual thinker is the emailer, the Auditory thinker is the voicemailer. They believe what they hear. So if you sent an email but didn't talk with them about it, they might miss it. After all, if it were important, you would've said so! They always check for confirmation with their auditory-out channel, by asking the same thing you just said. They'll say, "So, you're saying we're going for sushi first and then the movie?" and you'll say, "Well yeah, that's exactly what I said." It's not that they didn't hear you; it's just how they confirm what they got from

that Auditory-In channel. Just confirm it for them, and you're good to go.

Getting the words right is so important that you might notice an auditory communicator close their eyes or look away while they speak. This helps them focus their listening or speaking by shutting out all visual stimulus. This is amplified when it's important or an emotional situation. If you're visual (want someone to look straight at you), understand that their looking away is helping them to hear you better, not tune you out or not try to offend you.

Listen for sound effects.
An auditory processor makes actual sounds as they listen, "M-hmm," "uh-huh," "Right, right" as you talk to them. So, their processing comes out in a way you can hear. If you're brainstorming with an auditory thinker, know that they'll narrate their whole process, whereas somebody who's not auditory might just give you the idea, and then the next version of the idea without everything in between.

Internal dialogue is loud and important for auditory thinkers. Their little voice is a lot more participatory than somebody else's little voice. They're engaged in dialogue with that voice all the time. It's like another person in the room. In fact, a lot of times for auditory people it comes out, out loud, as they talk to themselves.

Auditory thinkers notice every surrounding sound and conversation. While an auditory person might love to listen to music while they work, if somebody else is playing music while they're working in a common space, they'll have to choose a focus for their listening. If somebody at the other end of the room is tapping a pencil, the auditory person will notice it, be bothered by it and probably say something about it.

Make it ring for them. Resonating with the *Auditory* thinker will roll off your tongue easier than you think. Here's how to harmonize with them 1:1...

1:1 with Auditory Alex::

- Sit next to her, in a place where she can hear you without competing conversations around you.
- Periodically (at the end of natural sections), ask her to tell you what she's heard so far (paraphrasing back) – this will help her process better by having it come out of her own mouth.
- Be sure to pace yourself, not talking too quickly.
- Go through your points sequentially- don't jump around.
- Suggest that she record the session, so she can have it and play it back later if she wants.
- When she's talking, don't interrupt- wait til she's done, then paraphrase what you heard back to her.
- Listen to and respond to her reactions to your points- she'll show her agreement and disagreement throughher "hmmph"s and "uh-huh"s
- Use phrases like: "listen", "I hear you", "it sounds like", "how does that sound", "do you hear what I'm saying","I'd like to say"
- Check in with her frequently with "how does that sound to you?" or "does that sound right to you?".
- Leave a follow-up voicemail for her, letting her know how great it was to hear her thoughts and talk.

Here's a quick cue card to reference as you're interacting with the Auditory thinkers already in your world, whether you've identified them yet or not. Experiment with these, and notice how some people will tune right in, hearing your every word...

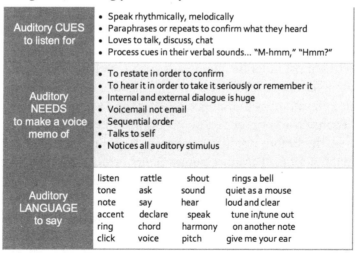

Auditory CUES to listen for	• Speak rhythmically, melodically • Paraphrases or repeats to confirm what they heard • Loves to talk, discuss, chat • Process cues in their verbal sounds... "M-hmm," "Hmm?"
Auditory NEEDS to make a voice memo of	• To restate in order to confirm • To hear it in order to take it seriously or remember it • Internal and external dialogue is huge • Voicemail not email • Sequential order • Talks to self • Notices all auditory stimulus
Auditory LANGUAGE to say	listen rattle shout rings a bell tone ask sound quiet as a mouse note say hear loud and clear accent declare speak tune in/tune out ring chord harmony on another note click voice pitch give me your ear

Kinesthetic

How are you feeling right this minute? Check in with yourself and pinpoint it.

You either went to how you are physically feeling (achy, energetic, hot, cold...) or you went to your *emotions* (happy, sad, confused...). Either one was kinesthetic. It's commonly misunderstood that Kinesthetic is just tactile and movement, but it actually includes emotional engagement too. As you do what you do moving through every day, you are using this modality. In Kinesthetic mode, you are active or resting, noticing how you physically or emotionally feel.

Despite anyone's preferred modality, Kinesthetic actually trumps the other modalities in memorability and engagement, every time.
Two reasons...

Flex muscle memory.
You know how to ride a bike. Yet if I told you that starting today you're not allowed to ride a bike for the next 10 years, and then the first day of the 11th year, I gave you a bike and said, "Okay, you can ride it now," would you know how to ride it? Of course you could, because it's in your muscle memory, which takes a lot to wipe out. So, we know it's in there.

Emotions stick.
Think of the most indelible memories you've had over your life. What pops out? Every time, it's the emotionally loaded ones. Our brains burn those into our memory more permanently than any others. This is partly because the very section of our brains that consolidates memories (the limbic system) is the same section that also processes emotional reaction. "Far more neural fibers project from our brain's emotional center into the logical/rational centers than the reverse, so emotion is often a more powerful determinant of our behavior than our brain's logical/rational processes."[4] The more you emotionally engage people, the more able you are to have all of their thinking in the mix and make lasting impact on them.

Combining these, if you can get people *emotionally engaged* in a positive way[5] **and** get them *moving*, you're IN!

As I made you do those motions for Visual, Auditory, and Kinesthetic at the beginning of this chapter, I got your physical AND your emotional, right?

That said, you've also got predominantly Kinesthetic processors in your world. Here's what you need to *get* about them...

A Kinesthetic person loves movement. They are emotionally driven more than other people are. Being comfortable physically and emotionally is critical in order for them to operate. They reside in their bodies and their feelings, not their heads. They pick up on where other people are, and are more sensitive than they want you to know.

They also have some language patterns... They usually speak slowly, with long pauses between thoughts (they're checking out how it feels before they say it). There might be a big pause, and then they'll say, "Hmm, here's what I'm sensing about that..." And they'll also say things like...

"Hmm, I really want people to **grasp** this idea."
"Here's what I **feel**."
"All right, just **hold** it. I **get** it."
"I really want you to **get in touch** with this idea."
"I don't know if people really **have a handle** on this as well as I'd like them to."
"Let's just **throw** some ideas around."
"I think we really need to **stir up** the process a little bit."
"Hmm, she doesn't **strike** me as the kind of person who will **gel** with the team."
"Let's just **move** through this as quickly as we can."
"I really want to **hit** the customer **hard** with this."
"We need to make some big **impact** on every single person on the team."
"I think we need to **sharpen** our tools just a little bit in this area."
"We want to make it as **tangible** as we can."

Feel it.
You might notice a Kinesthetic person in a meeting either fidgeting, or slumped into a posture that looks disengaged. Don't be misled...they're *with* you! They just have to be comfortable and also need to move, so whatever it takes for those to occur they will do, and then they can

focus like crazy. A visual person might be sitting up very straight, an auditory person might be leaning in toward you, so that they can really hear every little piece. But a Kinesthetic person might be lounging back, still totally with you. Their cues are visible from the neck down; if they're disgruntled they might be turned away or have folded their arms across their chest.

In order to really get ideas going, they need to manipulate things physically, they need to move, they need to actually *do something* with the idea. Give space for them to walk around or stand up. If you're in a brainstorming session, have toys like koosh balls in the space—the kinesthetic processors will be able to focus better and engage *further* in the conversation while they play with them (while more visual or auditory folks will just leave the toys alone). Their ideas will come easier and faster. They speak slowly, though, so stick with them for their deep insight.

Comfort is key. So, if they're stuck in a little cubicle in an uncomfortable chair it's going to completely affect the quality of their work. That's not good for anyone, but it will affect them faster than somebody else. Physical environment impacts our kinesthetic modality all the time, so pay attention to temperature, space, lighting, air flow, what people get to sit on, and flow of the actual work space. While your Kinesthetic processors are already aware of it, these all matter for them much more than aesthetics.

It *is* personal.
Kinesthetic thinkers only believe, remember and own what they connect with emotionally or physically. I've coached many Kinesthetic leaders who commonly get to, "I just have a gut feeling about this, so that's what we're going to do." That's Kinesthetic decision-making, and how they roll.

While you may approach things as "it's not personal," just know that it's all personal[6] for a Kinesthetic thinker. Relationship and connection are incredibly important in how they work. If they have any sense that you don't like them, forget having any impact with them. Worse yet, if they don't like you or sense that you're inauthentic, forget it. Build a relationship and make it personal for them, and you'll get their absolute best work, best ideas and all-in support. Sink it in for them. Connecting with the Kinesthetic processor will set you up. Here's how:

1:1 with Kinesthetic Katherine:

- Sit next to her, in a place where the physical surroundings feel comfortable for her (let her choose).
- Take a few minutes before you start to check in and see how she's feeling, doing, etc. personally.
- Make sure that you are personally connected before you begin.
- Tell her in the beginning what you're committed to out of the meeting (her getting to her best, etc).
- Let her hold her own copy of the notes as you go through it.
- Give her a little more time to process points before you move on to the next ones (she needs to check in with her feelings, then respond).
- Watch for and respond to her physical cues as you go- gestures, body language (crosses arms or pushes back if disagrees, leans forward if agrees).
- Don't rush- give the meeting plenty of time.
- Use phrases like, "I sense", "I get", "my feeling is", "what's your sense", "does that feel right to you", plus action words like "strike, impress, hit, impact, tap, initiate, move, throw, stir, grasp, get, handle..."
- Be sure to check in to see how she's feeling at the end, and bring it to closure in a positive way.
- End with a physical closure- a hug, high-five or handshake (whichever feels appropriate).

Here's your quick cue card to hold for Kinesthetic processors all around you. Try these on, and sense the difference in how some people will connect with you faster and deeper...

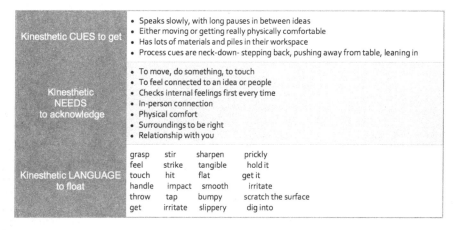

Kinesthetic CUES to get	• Speaks slowly, with long pauses in between ideas • Either moving or getting really physically comfortable • Has lots of materials and piles in their workspace • Process cues are neck-down- stepping back, pushing away from table, leaning in			
Kinesthetic NEEDS to acknowledge	• To move, do something, to touch • To feel connected to an idea or people • Checks internal feelings first every time • In-person connection • Physical comfort • Surroundings to be right • Relationship with you			
Kinesthetic LANGUAGE to float	grasp feel touch handle throw get	stir strike hit impact tap irritate	sharpen tangible flat smooth bumpy slippery	prickly hold it get it irritate scratch the surface dig into

Notes:

Visual 👀

auditory 👂

Kinestectic 🧍

- visual first then kinested

"...let go of your judgment, find a way to believe it's possible for them to excel, and coach to that gap between their performance and their potential."

Chapter 11:
More Power Than You Know

Think of a handful of people in your world (who work with you, for you, etc.) and line them up in rank order in your mind, as you think of them as the worst (1) to the best (10), with the following numbers over their heads...

1   2   3   4   5   6   7   8   9   10

That probably wasn't too hard. Because we do it every day; we humans are judgment machines. While you may actually need to rank your people's performance as part of your work, we do it in our heads anyhow, and it goes further than just performance. We put numbers over people's heads consciously or unconsciously, and then interact with them based on those numbers, which are a mashup of their skills, ability, attitude and how we feel about them overall. So, with somebody who you see as a "10," a superstar, you interact in a very specific way. With someone you see as a "1" or "2," you interact very differently. The way you interact has more to do with what's actually possible for each of these people than you think it does. One belief-shifting experience cemented this for me.

Life Learning
While I was teaching high school on the south side of Chicago, I got a student who ended up teaching me more about my own impact than anyone ever had before. She was a fourteen-year-old freshman named

Teresa whose reputation preceded her, in a bad way. She had a track record of having been kicked out of classes and schools, with horrible behavior, bad grades and a troubled home life. Every teacher who had her on their roster was warned to watch out, to not let her get away with anything. On that scale of 1 to 10, she was labeled a "0" before she even walked in the door=trouble.

Determined to do things differently (and skeptical of other teachers' judgments anyhow), I made a decision about Teresa before I ever met her. I was going to block out what I had heard about her. Whoever this kid was, I was going to make it my mission to find something in her they hadn't found yet. On a scale of 1 to 10, I was going to find the 10 in her. I was going to *Be the believer*, relentlessly holding that the "10" was possible, was in there.

Sure enough she arrived the first day of class, and displayed everything we'd been warned about. She had a bad attitude, horrible behavior, a foul mouth. She was disrespectful, started issues with other people, didn't listen; on a scale of 1 to 10, she was showing up as a minus 15. By the end of the first week of school, she was kicked out of every class in her schedule. *Except mine.*

It wasn't because her behavior was so different in my class—it wasn't. I just reacted differently than other teachers did. When she started with the attitude or was disrespectful and uncooperative, I chose to react in the same way I'd react to any *superstar* kid. I let her know clearly that the behavior she'd just *chosen* wasn't going to work in my classroom, but that I knew she had a lot of options to choose differently —always keeping it about the behavior and the choice she made, *not* about who she was. There were consequences, etc. just like other kids got, but I refused to kick her out of the class, and would always greet her the same way as she entered—looking her in the eye, smiling authentically and saying "Hey! I'm so glad you're here. Anything is possible today—let's go!"

Many days with her were really rough. But every now and then she would let herself slip. Despite herself, she would engage in an activity we were doing in class, would actually allow herself to enjoy it just a little bit, a smile would creep across her otherwise sour face, or she would say something to contribute. A couple times she actually said something brilliant, and everyone in class looked at her in shock. She then realized what she'd done, and the wall went right back up again. But those moments were immeasurable for me. They got me through the rough parts with her, and became the video clips I held in my head as I thought about and watched her choices in frustration. I superimposed those positive images over anything else I saw her do, so that every time she'd choose minus-five behavior I'd visualize the "10" moment overlay on top, and respond to *that* version of her. I just kept picturing the 10, responding to the 10, talking to the 10. Often, as she chose those negative paths over and over, I wondered if it was worth the inordinate energy I was putting into this approach. It would've been so easy to just snap back at her, and be done, and often took *a lot* of State-changing and Be-Do-Have-ing on my part to choose a different way.

I'll never forget a particular day, when things escalated. Teresa was very volatile, and would get set off easily. That day in class she was in a particularly irritated state, and I was particularly insistent that she participate in a group activity. She got incensed, so mad at me that she stood up and *threw a desk across the room at me* while screaming profanity at me.

It was as if time stood still in that moment. Every other student in the class froze, turned to see exactly how I was going to respond, and she stopped, poised in fighting position, ready to physically take me on. I took a breath, took a step back, checked my state and said, "Okay, you just made a choice that's not going to work in this room. So you've got to go now. But I want you to know that I respect that this was *your* choice to make this time. And anything's possible."

There was this pause of silence that felt like a year.

She looked at me with confusion, as if asking 'Did you not get what I just did?' I stood firm and repeated myself one more time, just so *she* really got what I was saying. She ended up needing to go with security, but I insisted with school administration that she *not* be suspended (as one normally would for a stunt like that), but come back to my class the next day.

The next day I stood in the doorway of my classroom, greeting kids as they came into my class like I did every other day. As Teresa approached, she was talking and laughing with her friends, and when she saw me her body language immediately changed. She switched into tough mode, guard up, ready for me to meet her at the door with a threat of "Don't even think about..." like every other teacher did.

Which I didn't do.

She got to the door, paused, and I said, "Hey, I'm glad you're here. Today anything's possible, and I look forward to what you choose. Let's go!" And I looked at her straight in the eye and smiled. She looked back at me with this look of "Wow, lady, you are from another planet," and walked into the room kind of keeping her eyeballs fixed on me suspiciously. She didn't cause trouble that day, and I kept treating her like the "10" I knew was in there somewhere. She had other outbursts and tested me regularly. Every single time I would stop, picture that "10" overlay, take a breath and react exactly the same way. Being the believer every day with her was exhausting.

Finally, we got to the end of the semester. Although I never changed the way I believed in her, by sheer points and grades Teresa had definitely failed the class. It was exam time, and I knew that one of a couple of things could happen. She would either completely sabotage the 90-minute final exam period (because she had nothing more to gain or lose), or she wouldn't. Either way, I knew that it was my last shot with here. How was I going to use it?

The night before her exam I was grading papers at my regular bookstore cafe hangout, thinking about what I wanted to do in my final 90-minute window with her to have the impact I had been shooting for all semester. I spotted one of those tiny 2"x 3" hardback inspirational quote books displayed near bookstore checkouts, bought it and wrote inside the cover: "Teresa, just so you know, I'll always believe in you... anything is possible. -Miss Singer." When she came in that next day for the exam, I silently slid that little book underneath her test, and never looked back. At the end of the period, she walked out and the book was gone, so I assumed that she took it. And as she walked out that day, I wondered to myself if I'd made any impact with her.

I spent the next few days between semesters grading exams, clearing my head, reset-ting for the impact I wanted to Have on this new batch of kids—what I'd Do, who I'd Be. When I came back to the new semester, guess who was there on one of my new class rosters. That's right—Teresa.

I thought, "Wow, am I up for this again? Here we go." I would be the relentless believer, no matter what.

It came time for her class. I stood there at the door greeting all of my new students, and then something crazy happened. I saw her coming down the hallway with her friends, and when she saw me...she broke into a run. *Toward me.* Then it was me thinking, "Is she crazy?" but I went with it. She had a smile on her face, and ran down the hallway to give me the biggest hug a kid has ever given me. "Ms. Singer! How are you? You're the greatest teacher in the world. I'm so glad I'm in your class again!"

A different version of Teresa showed up that day than had ever shown up in my class. She sat in the first row, told other kids in the class how great my class was going to be, how great I was (but not to mess with me). She went from being the troublemaker to the visible superstar. She raised her hand for everything, got other kids to participate and got on the troublemakers before I ever could.

At the end of that day, processing 150 new faces and names, new classes and what had happened with Teresa, I took a breath to sit down at my desk, which was full of debris. I noticed a wadded up ball of paper on the corner of my desk.

I picked it up to throw it away, but for some reason didn't and opened it instead.

It was a three-page double-sided, single-spaced, pencil-smudged letter that Teresa had written and left for me. "Dear Ms. Singer..." which went on about how I was the first person who had ever given her a chance, who didn't give up on her despite how she tried to block me out, the first person who ever believed in her, far beyond any way she ever believed in herself. In her own words she said, thank you for being the first person to think I'd be anything but dead or in jail by the time I was 18...my mom [who she'd lost when she was little] would be so proud...I was blown away. I sat there in my empty classroom and cried as I re-read that letter over and over, thinking back on how many times over those months I had almost given in to my frustration to react with her the way every other teacher did. I thought about what the cost would've been if I had. Being the relentless believer was worth the struggle.

That day I learned the power of In-10-tion...of ruthless commitment to someone's success no matter what...beyond what they show, and maybe beyond what they believe is possible in themselves.

I inspected every paper wad before I tossed it after that, and ended up with many letters she wrote to me, which I'd find in that same way. In them she shared what she was realizing about herself—that she acted that horrible way because it was all anyone expected.

It was easy for Teresa to be a minus 15. She was good at it, and nobody thought she could anything else, so why even try?[2] Yet at some point during the barrage of my re-lentless belief in her "10"[1] under there somewhere that semester, she realized that *something else* was possible—she actually could be more than she had been before. She could step into it and try it on. Teresa was different from then on, at least during those 52 minutes a day, five days a week in my classroom. She was a superstar in my class, was happy and engaged, and even got promoted to Honors English by the end of the semester once she showed herself what she could do. Yet my heart sank as I watched how easily she went right back into that old behavior in other classes, where other teachers held that low number over her head.

For the rest of her four years in school and beyond that, Teresa and I had many intense conversations in which I kept pushing what she knew she could do, and she struggled to step into it despite what other people thought. It was huge.

Right Here, Right Now
This isn't about Teresa. It's about everyone you influence with the numbers you silently have over their heads every day. You could have somebody like Teresa in your world. Maybe they're not such vivid case, but you have people right now with low numbers over their heads. My question to you as their leader—what is possible[3] for that person?

Researcher Robert Rosenthal first coined the idea of the "Pygmalion Effect"[4] in his re-search focused on the undisputable power of someone's belief from a leveraged position like a coach, manager or leader and the person has over our self-efficacy. Over 300 separate studies have been done on this topic by a myriad of researchers across work, education, sports and even law performance over a few decades.

In looking at what ultimately determines someone's level of performance or mastery...all the skill, motivation and experience that performer brought to it might only be **equal** to what the *coach thought they could do.*

So, even if this person had a ton of skills, knowledge, experience, motivation, inspiration...if the coach thought they couldn't do it, they ultimately wouldn't be able to do it.

So, if you have somebody who's got all of the pieces in place, but you've got a "3" over their head, they're never going to be more than that number. I can't even tell you how many people I've seen who have been held back by a number that somebody else was holding over their head. Professionals, students, athletes, identities.

You Get It
Think of a time in your life (as an adult or as a kid), when somebody had a low number over your head. Go there for a minute. How did you know? Did they ever have to say it out loud?

Even if they did, you already knew, right? How did it affect you? Likely, you felt like there was nothing you could do to get past it. You lost motivation, questioned your own ability[5], maybe even made stupid mistakes, right? Hopefully, you got out of there.

Now think of the opposite...a time when someone had a "10" over your head—thought you were a superstar. How did that impact you? It felt great, right? You may have even tapped into more ability than you previously thought you had, just because they believed in you.

You were inspired, confident...all the difference to be able to put yourself out there and show what you knew, right?

You are having **both** *kinds of impact on people right now*, whether you intend to or not. You have high numbers and low numbers over their heads. And they know it. You don't have to ever say it out loud, because it's already coming through in everything you do with them. In my own observation of thousands of coaches, teachers, managers and leaders in multiple settings...it's obvious. We can watch a teacher teaching an honors class, then a remedial level class and it's as if *they're* a different person. In the honors class, they speak faster, use a bigger vocabulary, are lighter in tone, are more entertain-ing and engaging. With the remedial class, they speak slower and louder (as if the students are deaf), they're much more serious, their body language is stiff, and they're boring and unengaging. Same person, dramatically different teaching that lower class, "2's" over every one of those kids.

The Stakes
Everyone has a "10" in them in some way, in some capacity.
Unless you can find and speak to the 10 in every person who reports to you, let them go.
Literally, let them go report to somebody else, in some other place.

I know that's a strong statement, yet it's critical for the lives you're impacting right now. Because it doesn't matter how gifted or talented they are, if *you* can't see the 10 in them, it will never come out, and *everybody deserves the opportunity to be the superstar they could be and have a leader who believes in their possibility.*

I've coached so many situations in which someone was about to be fired because their performance or attitude was so bad... but then transformed into a superstar when we just moved them to a different leader who believed in what they could do. We see this in work teams, sports teams and life teams.

To be clear, just because you put a 10 over somebody's head, it doesn't mean that their skills are going to change overnight. They won't. Yet as you start looking to find greatness and talent in them that you weren't seeing before, they'll feel it and it'll start to come out. Dr. Barbara Fredrickson's research confirms that "positive emotions...broaden people's ideas about possible actions, opening our awareness to a wider range of thoughts."[6] But the longer they've had that 2 over their head, the longer it might take you both to believe there's a 10 up there. You have to see it first. To get there, you may need to take mental snapshots of their great moments, and use the overlay method I used with Teresa.

Or let go of that thing they screwed up two years ago, which you're still hanging onto.
Or listen to some of their ideas you've been dismissing.
Or try looking at them as you do your superstar.

The more you start committing to what's possible in them and letting them know that you're not letting up, the more they'll start considering themselves differently and performing. I've heard managers trying this out complain that "no matter how many times I put a "10" over a person's head, *they keep knocking it* down to a "3" again with their performance and attitude."
Those managers are *missing the point.* It's not about performance.

Coach it.

It could be that their performance is a "3." That doesn't mean that you see *them* as a "3." You treat and see them as their potential 10, then **coach to the gap**—*that difference between their potential and their performance.* When I was teaching, I always told my students (especially the lowest level ones), "How many of you know that you're way smarter and more talented than people think you are? [Of course they'd agree.] You know it's in there. I know it's in there. Our mission here is to show the world it's in there in the way you demonstrate it every day."

So, I've called out the big elephant in their existence, maybe even the source of their angst or attitude, if they have one—that *gap.* Once it's known, we can address it and I can coach it directly. I've given my vocal commitment to push their performance and give them whatever coaching it takes. And then I don't let up. Yet because I'm coming from a commitment to their possible "10" as my agenda (vs. expecting them to fail), I've got the grounding to be able to coach them hard—**Be**ing the Believer, with that ruthless commitment to their success. When they know that you believe in their possibility, they'll let you push. And you should, not letting them settle for less than their best.

It's all you, coach.
I say, "I'm committed to your success, and I know you've got more in you than this pro-ject showed, which didn't hit it. Let's figure out how to get what you've got in you up and out to crush this." and then I deliver pointed, specific coaching about how it needs to improve.

Call it.

So does this mean that you just keep someone on indefinitely who's not performing, hoping they come around to the "10" you've never seen? No. It means that you have to let go of your judgment, find a way to believe it's possible for them to excel, and *coach to that gap* between their performance and their potential. A lot.

If you honestly do that with pure In-10-tion, and nothing improves, then you call it as the wrong fit. Either you're the wrong leader for them, or this position is the wrong fit for their talent. People end up in the wrong jobs/positions for their talents all the time. If this is one of those cases, help them find the right fit where they can be awesome. Some of the most empowering conversations I've had with people were the ones where I let them go, because it was still coming from that ruthless commitment to their success. I'm committed to their success as a person, and if my team isn't the place for them to fulfill that 100%, then I want them to go find the place that is—because they deserve that shot!

Try this...

Imagine, if you would, two people in your mind. Somebody who is your absolute superstar, like 10, off the charts even. And then think of somebody else who reports to you, who is a really low number. Let's say a one, a two, a three, a four, okay?
Hold those two people up in your mind side by side.

Take one: Let's just say that you give your superstar some kind of task which they completely botch. How would you respond to that person? You'd probably give him a little grace, wouldn't you? "Okay, wow, that was bad, but let's see -- let's see how we can retrace our steps. Let's see if we can go back and put the pieces together. Let's see how we can set you up, so that that doesn't happen again. Let me give you some coaching. Let me walk it through with you...." right?

Take two: Go back to the other person who has the really low number over their head. Now let's just say you give him the exact same task, and he botches it completely. How would you respond to that person? Way different, right? You'd respond impatiently, might fly off the handle. Or you expected them to screw up in the first place, so it's just one more reason why that person deserves a four, right? None of the coaching, the walking them through to retrace steps. So... what's the only difference between Take one and Take two? You. Your response. The number you have over their heads, which either opens the whole thing up to forward motion or closes it down along with their possibility. That's all you, boss.

Think about this and the numbers you have over people's heads— at work, in your family, in your life. They're not going to change overnight, but until you believe the 10 is in there and speak to it, it'll never come out. **You** have the power to find, inspire and bring out their greatness. Choose to.

Notes:

"Remember that microscope you're under all the time... You don't get the luxury of being sloppy about saying one thing, but doing something else, because when you do, you lose your right to influence them."

Chapter 12:
The Three Ingredients

*What if you could find the "10" in that one person who you've struggled
with for so long?*
What if they actually wanted you to coach them?
*What if you had the secret combination to unlock rapport with anybody,
and actually could be able to step into that coaching role to influence and
inspire them—rather than just manage them?*

An inspiring coach is able to make contact with somebody right where
they are, reach inside and pull out their greatness, so that person can
just step into it and take action. We'd all like to have that kind of
influence with anyone, right? Yet it seems kind of superhero-ish and
unattainable when you're considering someone whose head you've
had a "2" over, or someone with whom you have conflict or no rapport,
doesn't it?

Good news. What those inspiring coaches do consistently and what
you already do unconsciously with the folks you already have
influence with actually has a recipe to it, with specific ingredients you
can manually add to the mix. It doesn't have to feel so mysterious.

One way to understand it is in seeing the contrast of your dynamic with
someone you love working with (maybe that superstar from the last
chapter) against someone you can't stand working with (maybe that
low-numbered person from the last chapter). Side by side, there are a
couple of big differences.

Can you hear me now?
There are only two worlds that matter in coaching and influence
—Yours and Theirs. When you have natural rapport with someone,
those two worlds meet somewhere. With something in common,
something uniquely understood, a connection opens up and your
worlds start to align and ideally overlap. When you don't have rapport
—either because you lost it or you never established it in the first place

—your two worlds feel distinctly separate, almost unable to touch. It's like a phone call with good or bad reception. With a solid connection, what you're saying is strong, clear and getting through; with a spotty connection, it's a struggle to hear you, and what you're saying never really gets through.

Most likely, your connection is already established with those folks you love working with, maybe in multiple ways. Your worlds connect. You get them and they get you. They're listening.

But with those low-numbered folks, you have a static-y connection at best. Whether your worlds are similar or different, they're definitely far away from one another. They might hear you shouting to them from all the way over in your world, but there's not enough connection to make out the details. And they don't really care enough to move around until there's better reception. Meanwhile, you may have gotten tired of shouting the same thing over and over, so maybe stopped trying. Worlds apart, no connection.

Influence

Simply put, influence is about something or someone getting into my head that shifts how I think, feel, see or decide. When it comes down to it, whose choice is it for you to influence or even inspire someone? *Theirs.*

Short of threatening situations, nobody gets to sway our thinking unless we allow them into our heads, right? You can tell when someone has allowed you in, is considering it, or has shut you out, because they're giving you signs all the time. When you have a good connection, that influence is there and happens easily. When you don't, the door of influence is closed.

Sometimes leaders tell me "It doesn't matter if they want to listen to me. Because I'm their boss, they have to. They don't have to like me."

That's manager-speak. And technically true—they don't *have* to like you to do their jobs, but if you want their alliance and a shot at inspiring their awesomeness vs. just their compliance, then they also need to choose to allow you into their heads. *First, Break All the Rules* is the summation of one of the most importantly revealing studies[1] in leadership done by the Gallup Poll; it showed that across industries the single-most influential factor determining people's choice to perform, go above and beyond expectation and have longevity to the work wasn't pay, company benefits, mission or other elements. It was their relationship with their direct boss. If everything else was great, but that relationship wasn't, their performance suffered, and they didn't last. Makes sense with In-10-tion, right?

So, to have *both* authentic connection *and* influence, it's actually more straightforward than you think, because when you build it naturally you're unconscious about it. So, let's consciously, intentionally build some connection and inroads into their heads, so you can tap the greatness in there.

It actually just comes down to three ingredients...

Ingredient #1: Enter their world

Have you ever worked for someone who didn't seem to care or know anything about your world? It was all about work, and the idea that you had a life outside of it never even got acknowledged? How much were you willing to do for somebody like that? My guess is that you did what was required, but not much more. The farther apart our worlds are, the easier it is to stay disengaged. The more I think you don't care about my world, the less I care about what's important to you in your world, and I'm not going to let you in to any of my greatness, because you don't get me anyhow. So I'd rather just keep my greatness secret and intact to myself, and play small with you.

Their motivation, priorities, talent and potential all live in their world —so you've got to get in there. The first step is to get out of yours.

Little Ways

If someone busted into your house through your bathroom window instead of knocking on the front door, you wouldn't be so excited to engage with them, would you? Yet you've had moments of busting into someone's world to tell them to do something without first acknowledging what was going on in their world, only to be met by bad re-sults or no results at all, right? You expect them to drop whatever they're doing and come over to where you are—to your agenda, your priorities, your world.

They might be willing if you metaphorically knocked on their door first. Getting kicked out of their heads vs. being invited in.

The basic level of this process: as you approach, check out where they are. Ask. "Hey—I see you're in the midst of something. What are you working on? Do you have a minute?" (knock. knock.)

But it's also in the multiple doors you can knock on...

- speak and lead in their language
- make them a partner
- check in with them as people before directing them
- ask about their lives
- tell them what you love about their work and why you appreciate them
- tap into their WHY
- ask their input
- give them a partnership role
- use their ideas
- create opportunities for them to tap their own uniqueness and creativity
- trust them and earn their trust
- ask their input
- acknowledge them consistently, and what they are contributing

The Introvert-Extrovert part matters.

Where you fall on the introvert-extrovert spectrum[2] has something to do with how you're naturally connecting with some people more easily than others. I believe that very few people are 100% introvert (get all your energy from being alone, tend to be much more inward) or extrovert (get energy from interaction with others, tend to be much more out-ward), yet most of us are definitely a bit skewed one way or another. Blazing loudly in command mode, into a more introverted person's world is the equivalent of busting through their bathroom window again. Conversely, waiting for a more extroverted to just keep their ideas to them-selves and listen quietly during a whole meeting will just give you more validation for a "2" over their head, because they won't do it. As Daniel Pink points out, "Ambiverts can find that balance. They know when to speak up and when to shut up."[3] So if you're Entering the world of someone more introverted, do more asking than telling, skip the small talk, and let them think about what you're asking before they respond. If you're entering an extroverted world, lean in, speak up, and dive in.

Get personal.
How often do you go into the world of that low-numbered person? Likely not very often. You might even be avoiding their world altogether.

This piece is challenging for many. You may have been taught to keep business and professional completely separate. "Don't make it personal. Don't get involved in their lives. Don't get involved with who they are." That's manager-speak, left over from old-school, ends-justify-*any*-means[4] management. You don't need to be best friends with them, but you do need to build connection with them in order to have influence, which will occur only when they get that you care, in their world.

They want you to care about them just as much as they want you to care about the work they do.

Test: For each of the folks on your team, do you know what they like to do during their time off? If they have a significant other? If so, their name? Do they have any kids? If they do, how old are they? What are their names? If you can't answer those questions, it's a flag that you haven't really entered their world. There's a correlation between who you know those answers about and who you've already got connection, isn't there? With the oth-ers, ask the questions, and you'll start to build it! This might mean rewiring what you've been taught. The more you enter their world -> the more rapport you'll establish-> the more trust you'll build, the more loyalty you'll gain -> and greatness you'll tap.

> **Real Influencer moment:**
> One retail leader I know who tried this was uncomfortable, yet amazed. She had a colleague with whom she was always at odds, and everyone had written off as a curmudgeon with whom no progress could be made. She really needed him as a partner in the strategy she was trying to roll out. Our leader really wanted to break through, and was determined to get him to open up. She knew that he was an Ohio State football fan (and so was she); when he talked about Buckeye football, he was relaxed, animated, and engaged. So she started there. She intentionally stopped approaching him with strategic work things, and just talked with him about Buckeye football. It became their connection- their shared world. Each Monday she'd find him and they'd debrief the weekend's game, coaching and performance. By the end of that football season, she had developed ease and dialogue with him, and earned his trust.
>
> She re-introduced the business strategy, and he was all-in as her greatest partner!

Bring purpose.
Do you know why are they doing this work? What they really care about in it and what they want to cause in the world? Find out[5] if you don't know already. Once you can put their work into context of their total world, you both become more vested in its success. Create opportunities for them to tap into their own uniqueness and creativity. Partnership roles. Input. So, even if it's something that you're asking them to do, have them do it in such a way that they get to bring what they're good at. And you get to see more of what's great in their world.

Ingredient #2: Earn the right
Have you ever worked for somebody who you didn't truly respect? There's nothing worse. If you've had a low number over their head, their pride hasn't allowed them to respect you. And for that permission into their heads, you've got to earn it. Get this, and they're onboard with you, listening, greatness tapped and delivering. Don't and they're still on the dock, holding back, resisting.

And to earn it, be real...
Do they really care how many years you've been doing this? No.
Do they care how many degrees you have? No.
Do they really care how much money you make? No.

Do they even care about your position, in their heart of hearts? Not really.
They care about whether or not you've earned their respect, which gives you credibility, and the right to influence them.

The more you enter their world, the more you can earn the right. Try...

- build relationship with trust and partnership
- listen to them
- teambuild
- walk your talk
- share who you are with them
- find out who they are as a person
- share personal goals
- trust them and earn their trust
- use their ideas
- acknowledge them consistently, and what they are contributing

Walk your talk.
Because when you don't, the cleanup is ridiculous. To you it may be one little moment in which you said one thing, but did another. To them, it's your hypocritical lack of credibility, which they hold onto, tell other people all about, and it becomes your reputation. Remember that microscope you're under all the time; there are standards you're held to by reason of your position that don't apply to others. You don't get the luxury of being sloppy about saying one thing, but doing something else, because when you do, you lose your right to influence them.

Share more.
Actually share who you are as a person. I'm not saying pour out your heart and soul to them or tell your deepest darkest secrets. Yet do they know what you like to do when you're not at work, if you have a significant other in your life, if you have kids or not, and if so, their names?? When you share these things about yourself, you earn respect with them as a real human being just like they are—not just this role

that you play at work. They may not relate to you as a leader, but they can relate to you as a fan of the local basketball team or as a brother/ sister, a mother/father or significant other to someone. It allows your realities to come closer together somehow.

Share personal goals.

Tell them why you're doing this. What's your Big Why[6]? Where did you start? What's the next thing for you? They'll get that you're not just a role, but a dynamic human being with a history, present and future in the works all the time, just like them. It gives them some access to you in a relationship, on the same human playing field.

Trust is clutch.

Once you throw something out there, it's heard as a promise. Maybe you just said it in passing, but they'll expect it as a commitment you made; so either fulfill on it or clean it up immediately if you can't. Cleanup means vocally take ownership for it, apologize for the confusion if there is any, and recommit to reset expectations realistically. Trust them, and you earn their trust. Trust that they will deliver, and when they do acknowledge it, "Great, I trust you. I'm counting on you. Thanks for delivering."

Acknowledge them.

It's so easy to point out what they need to work on, and skip saying "Here's why you're so awesome. Here's what I love about what you just did. Here's how our team would not be where it is without what you've done." How often do you do that? In the last week? Even today? More with the high-numbered folks than the low-numbers, right? We leave the things people do well as the standard, and just assume that they know the value of it. A little acknowledgement goes really far to earn you the right as a leader who *gets it and values them*. Of course, this includes that input you just started asking for, too! You don't have to use every idea, but each time you ask, it sends a really clear message that you respect their thinking, their ideas, and their contribution, which earns you the right to get into their heads.

Earning the right to lead them as people, not just manage them as roles, and earning the right to be their inspiring, influential coach, not just their boss, is a *continual thing*. Often leaders mistakenly just earn the right in the beginning, and then *assume it* after that. You can *never* assume the right, because there's always a part of them who's searching for the chink in your armor. Keep earning it over and over.

Ingredient #3 Tap their WIIFM

We've already established the value of WIIFM[7] as the strongest motivator for any one person at any time. If they know what's in it for them, they'll listen, they'll take action, they'll make it their own, because they'll have a personal investment in success.

The more you enter their world, the more accurately you can tap their WIIFM, because you then know what's important to them, right? The more you earn the right, the more they hear the WIIFM as pure, rather than as a sales job to get them to do what you want them to do (which it should never be). And the more you tap their WIIFM, the more it earns you the right with them! See how these work together?

Specifically tap their WIIFM if you haven't yet:

- give your request some meaning and significance in their world
- give them a reason to WANT to do it for themselves- not just for you
- ask yourself "What's going on in this person's world right now?"and start the conversation from there
- share your perspective, but ask from their perspective
- create an opening for success for them within your request
- tell them what they could do to get even better instead of what they did wrong
- give them more personal incentives in addition to the company incentives

Your World Into Theirs

Give your request some meaning and significance in their world.
What's important to you in their execution of your request might be very different from what's important to them. So, think about how it will play out in their world, and how it can be big there.

Share your perspective, but ask from their perspective, in their language. So, let's say I'm talking with the team about staying late tonight. From my perspective, it's all about getting the project done (we have a client waiting!). From their perspective, it's about staying an hour later than they wanted to, eating into their personal time. Sounds like this, *"Hey you guys, we want to get out of here as soon as we can, right? And we also have this client waiting for our deck. So, let's brainstorm for a minute. How can we do this in a way that utilizes our time to crush this and also gets us out of here in the fastest possible way, to give everyone as much possible time on our own as we can?"*

All about Them
Find and create openings for success for them within your request. "Hey, Sam—what if *you could be the one* to make this presentation the thing that blows them out of the water?" There's always a way to shine a light on the contribution they're making, but you just might be skipping over it. Shine it and call it out.

Tell them what they could do to get even better instead of what they just did wrong. Language is so powerful. In giving people two-parted feedback we usually deliv-er the positive first before the negative. The receiver only partially hears that positive, because they're waiting for the "but..." that comes afterward with the bad news, replacing whatever you just said, and becoming their focus. If you really need to call out both, start with that commitment to their success first, so they get that your agenda is their greatness, not their failure. Yet more often than not, you don't really need to call out both. A simple change of wording changes the whole thing.

For example, I might have said, *"I really love the way that you led that meeting—people were into it because you had a lot of energy about it and were really clear. But it was a miss to not have handouts—you should have them. People had nothing to refer to later, and they walked away with no reference."* The first positive gets replaced by the negative.

Instead, try, *"I really love the way that you led that meeting—people were into it because you had a lot of energy about it and were really clear. And to make it even better make sure they have handouts next time, so that they can follow along as they go and they can also have something to refer to later."*

Replace "but" with "and," then tell them how to make it better. It flows together as all pos-itive, even though there was an opportunity there. They stay with you, listening through the whole thing, because you're setting them up for more success rather than buttering them up to hear the criticism.

Give them a reason to want to do it for themselves, not just for you. Corporate incentives are always around. Yet research[8] has proven that intrinsic motivation is way more powerful than the sweetest carrot you could dangle or the sharpest stick you could use to threaten. External reward systems can actually do more damage than good over time. For somebody who actually enjoys what they're doing already, if we dangle a reward in front of them to do it faster and better, they usually do accelerate and improve at first. But then, when the reward goes away, a horrible thing happens. They end up disliking the very behavior you tried to improve, which they liked in the first place! Now you've corrupted their original motivation. Steer clear.

Acknowledgement, autonomy, mastery and purpose all work powerfully. Leaving a post-it note on someone's laptop while they're at lunch that says, "Thank you so much for your contribution in our meeting today—it turned the whole thing around," or a public shout-out at the next department meeting can go really far. Some people prefer public praise, others prefer private. Find out which works best for your people, and give the acknowledgement to them in that form.

They get that they're appreciated, that they add value, that what they do matters. As you mess with these three ingredients, they'll start to get all over one another.

ENTER.
EARN.
TAP.

The more you Enter, the more you can Tap.
The more you Tap, the more you Earn.
Reception gets clearer, worlds get into alignment and you find their "10."

Even better, connection is made, communication becomes pure and clear, and influence happens.

You're in, where you can get and inspire their greatness.

Notes:

"The deepest level of individual personal drive we all have is our Big Why...why we're doing this in the great scheme of life. This is our biggest game, truest purpose, greatest good and what gets us out of bed in the morning."

Chapter 13:
The Pyramid of Perspective

What if you could be that leader who is the calm in the storm, the one who elevates the game even when things are crazy, the one who inspires people beyond the task at hand

Yet how many times have you gotten sucked into the stress of someone else's timeline or mak-ing sure the details of the steps were exactly right? This occurs on teams and in leadership dai-ly, and perspective gets lost. You want to channel the brilliance of your team while continually keeping perspective on their process. Think of it like a pyramid[1]...

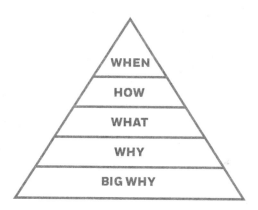

So, where's your vantage point? Each of the levels on this pyramid represents a different view-point or perspective. In the way that you lead and communicate, you can come from any of those levels, each one coloring your message and influence differently. The deeper you go on the pyramid, the broader your view becomes of all the layers, the more grounded perspective you bring to the team. As a leader, you've got some choices...

When

Picture yourself standing on the side of that pyramid, feet planted on the top layer of When. From there, you lose sight of those layers below you, and When becomes your orientation to everything. You've worked for or with someone like this before, and you get pushed there your-self when you're under the gun. *When* your boss is consistently coming from *When*, it's stressful, unfulfilling and feels never-ending, because as soon as something's done you see the stop-watches counting down on everything else. Coming from this place, you're all about your calendar, the team's schedule and deadlines and time (usually never enough). To be clear, time and When you deliver what you promise is critical. For a competitive team, *When* is an important and effective driver for them to get their work out there and come together before another tea beats them to it. High achievers often do their best work under pressure, so time and an impending constraint of *When* can bring out their best. Yet *When* can't become what it's all about, or you'll fry your people and yourself. That rush of adrenaline that comes in the 11th hour can be awesome, but only if you can recover afteward.

As my friend Tony Schwartz teaches us in *The Way We're Working Isn't Working: The Four Forgotten Needs That Energize Great Performance*,[2] we're built as humans to be able to sprint and then recover, not keep sprinting to marathon distances as we often attempt. As a leader, you can leverage *When* as a motivator without becoming the watch-checker. If you cross that line to become overly con-cerned with *When*, your team can dismiss you as valuing time over their content or quality in the process.

Keep *When* in perspective:
- **"We are here" on the map.**
  Just like finding the "X" on the map at the mall to see where you are in relation to where you need to go, there's peace of mind that comes in the present-moment orientation of our work to the Why. Build and show timelines to give your team a sense of how their process will play out in concrete terms, and then keep marking visually where you are in it, phase by phase.
- **Flex.**
  Adjust the timeline as you go, making space for their emergent process as they collaborate.
- **Spark.**
  Strategically use time and deliverables to create urgency when *needed*. Deadlines spur action.

How

Stepping a level deeper on the pyramid, *When* is still in view, but relative to *How*- better. Here, the focus is on the process, the steps and the way we get there. It's critical, because *How* your team does its magic may be the very thing that sets you apart from your competitors and defines your brand. Yet if you're overly skewed on form and checking off every box just so, they'll feel micromanaged, without enough choice or creativity. The trick is to get the Hows in place to tap into and *showcase* their talent, not ever *stifle* it.

If you've got a team of experts or individuals coming from successful yet diverse disciplines and experiences, the *How* will be important to them. They can get stuck on *How* your team is approaching the work, attached to a particular process to achieve results from their previous world. I've seen potentially brilliant teams crumble because they couldn't get aligned on process. *How* your team goes about its impressive impact is ultimately your call as the leader.

Keep *How* in perspective:
- *Be the keeper of the process.*
  Direct the approach, honoring and incorporating their expertise, then getting their buy-in on why X is the best way for the team. As the leader, either lead the collaboration to define process, or make the call yourself.
- *Check in early and often.*
  Get alignment on the *How* of your process early, check in and adjust course often, looking to make sure the *How* is tapping their talent consistently and providing a way for it to manifest in great work.

What

Great managers come from *How*—they focus us on the concrete thing we're trying to accomplish. This is the outcome—the impact we want to *Have* out of the work. Standing on this level, grounded in the *What*, *How* we'll go about it and by *When* that'll happen are now in proper perspective. Much better.

Keep *What* in perspective:

- ***Focus the picture.***
  Get clear on *What* your team is going for. The more inputs there are in the mix, the more important everyone's alignment on what we're creating and what impact we intend to have becomes. Articulate the primary goal as the leader, so they hear if from you.

- ***Tap Their WIIFM.***
  Have the team articulate the goal, too, and then have them build on it, identifying what impact they each want to have as a result of the work.

- ***Get the box lid visible.***
  Once it's clear, make it visible for everyone to keep looking up at, to refocus their work. Get it visually up in the workspace, and keep reiterating it for them.

- ***Call it where you can.***
  If the result you're going for is ambiguous, set shorter-term. What milestones along the course for them to focus on and hit on the way. "By the end of this week, here's *what* we'll *have* out of this process...."

Why

This is where you cross over from good manager to great *leader*. All the layers of the pyramid are key to keeping your team and the work focused on the right things at the right times. Yet the *Why* both trumps and grounds everything on that pyramid, because it gets to the pragmatic, problem-solving nature of our thinking and to the heart of human motivation. The *Why* of your work could be what brought them all onboard with you in the first place—a mission to _____ (fill in accordingly). It's their cause, their call, their drive— answering a bigger internal question for them. It brings it all back to purpose, which is energizing, clarifying and even calming. For you as the leader, getting the Team *Why* clear and articulated is the most important thing of all, after which everything else (What, How and When) is about execution. This is the conviction that makes the game matter, and the impact of their efforts bigger in the world. It's what engages these individual brilliant people on your team, bring-ing their separate *Whys* and visions of what's possible in the world to their work together. For ambiguous work where the "you are here" map keeps changing, this is even more important—keep re-orienting everyone to that *Why* so they have a reason to go forward into the unknown.

Layers of Why

In any moment of decision, there may be multiple levels of *Why*. You don't always need to call them out, but as a leader keep them straight in your head, ready to call out the ones necessary at the time, so everyone can orient accordingly.

It might look like this for a single simple decision to take down and redesign the signage and traffic flow in a restaurant:

- ***Tactical Why***—explains reaction to something that just happened or a problem that needs solving
  "Because our guests are getting confused about where they're supposed to go to place orders."
- ***Strategic Why***—explanation for what we know this will lead to or what we want to make happen
  "Because we want turnover time to go faster, and orders to be fast."
- ***Company Why***—for the organization, this is why it's important
  "Because here at SingerEats we're all about making the dining experience easy, enjoyable and focused on the food for our guests."
- ***Team Why***—for our team and what we want to cause in the world, this is why we're here
  "Because this team's all about being flexible and making the fastest, best decisions for our guests, to make their experience better."
- ***Personal Why***—for you personally (and them), this is what's important
  "Because I personally like it better this way."

As a leader, you want to answer all the layers of *Why* that exist in a particular scenario. Sort and prioritize them, deciding which one/s will help your team most in the moment to understand, get it quickly and jump in with you.

Keep *Why* in perspective:

- ***Lead your team with the Why.*** Tell the *Why* first. Ask the *Why*.

Every time, every conversation, every day.
- ***Open with the Why.*** (you decide how many layers) every single time. They're already asking the question in their heads, and if you don't answer it, they will, and it'll likely be inaccurate and negative[3] ("Why is he asking me to do this? Because he thinks I have nothing else to do?"). Then layer the What, How and When on top—*in that order.*

The BIG Why

Then we go way deeper, and to the core of it all. The deepest level of individual personal drive we all have is our Big Why... why we're doing this in the great scheme of life. This is our biggest game, truest purpose, greatest good and what gets us out of bed in the morning. ***Steve Jobs:*** "To make a dent in the universe."

This is what makes great leaders the kind who people want to rally with, dig deep for and follow- because it's about something way bigger. Remember what Daniel Pink taught us? Purpose[4] is one of the big three human drivers—getting to be part of something bigger than myself—a Big Why.

Your Big Why

As a leader, get clear about your own personal Big Why. Beyond your role, Why do you get out of bed in the morning to do what you do? You could hold lots of positions in lots of places. What supersedes them all? The opportunity to _____ every day for the sake of _____. Once you get clear about that, it will come through as the passion that fuels everything else you do, and will serve as inspiration for every person you lead. You may need to mine a bit beneath your first answer here.

Think of it as peeling the layers[5] back on the onion of your Big Why, getting down to your most fundamental Big Why beneath.

Layer-peeling to Your Big Why
Whatever your first answer is, follow it by asking yourself why that's important. Then ask yourself why that new thing is important to you... etc. I find that going five layers of that questioning beneath your first answer usually gets to *the big one.*

Once you're grounded in this deepest, most stable part of the pyramid, the others—WHAT, HOW, and WHEN—are easy to reference and command as needed, because they're truly held.

Simon Sinek became a viral sensation in 2009 with his TED talk about how leaders inspire action. He hit a nerve for us all, getting to Why as the most important influencer of our decisions. He reminds us that "those who lead inspire us, because we believe what they believe."[6] People followed Martin Luther King not because he proposed a great plan, but because he led with "I believe" the Why.

Their Big Why

If you know their individual Big Why, you have a very powerful way to connect with your people where it matters most, and help them tap what's possible in everything else they do. With it, you can frame communication—an entrance into what matters most in their world, despite the momentary What/How/When at hand. When they're in need of motivation, acknowledgment or perspective, you can frame it in the most meaningful way for what matters most to them. Their *Why* is their buy-in.

Their Layers

As you ask, know that these questions are the kind that may require people to search a little internally for if they haven't already clarified it for themselves. Give them space to think about it and then ask in layers...

You may ask them, "So why do you do this?"

They may say, "because I'm intrigued by X kinds of challenges," or some other such practical but notmeaningful answer.

You then follow up simply with,

"Why are these kinds of challenges intriguing to you?"

They might answer, "Because I really care about X..."

You probe, "Why do you care so much about X?"

...until you've asked five layers into their Why.

Find the Big Whys for each on your vital team by asking them (for some, the Big Why is already really clear, so you might not need all five layers). While this gets to what's most essential to people's core, many don't talk much about it or even think of it consciously to the level of easy articulation. So helping them to unearth it can be pivotal— enabling them to get personal clarity that expands their game and shifts everything. Then in your work together, they can tap into more connected passion about what they're doing, while you lead them more meaningfully toward their biggest impact and game.

Standing in and starting with the perspective of Big Why as the foundation, you can layer, reference and pull from those other Layers of Why, What, How and When easily, without getting sucked into them and losing your overall view.

Total Perspective
Your perspective colors how you choose, lead and relate to everyone around you, so keep yourself grounded. The art of it is to keep adjusting your vantage point for yourself and your team. When, How, What, Why are each important in different ways, can demand their own hy-per focus, and can consume you if you're not careful.

The deeper you go on the pyramid, the better your perspective is, able to reach and access each of the other levels in relation to the biggest picture. And you become the leader who clarifies and illuminates perspective for everyone else, no matter what gets thrown their way.

I know hundreds of leaders who at this very moment are carrying around a little mini version of the *Pyramid of Perspective* in their planner, wallet or phone as a reminder to get grounded in the 'why' of whatever they're doing and leading at the moment. Draw your own, and keep putting those layers back in order.

Because it's *all* about perspective.

Notes:

"This is counter to how most of us were taught, yet exactly how we actually learn in real life."

Chapter 14:
Making It Stick

*How much time have you spent re-teaching information or skills you've already taught? What if they could get it the **first** time, completely engaged, and it stuck?*

Part of being a leader means teaching and coaching, right? You're doing this all the time. Of course, we have specific times during training or rolling out something new when we do so really directly and in a focused, organized way. Yet you're constantly helping people get their skills more refined and take on new ones, to improve their performance and capacity.

You can accelerate how quickly people learn what you teach, reduce the time you're spending re-teaching and get them involved in a way they haven't been before, excited to learn from you.

Coaching to teach is an art unto itself. It seems like it *should b*e as simple as telling someone how to do something. It feels faster to give them the answers or simply tell them what results they need to deliver, but that *doesn't* get them there, and slows their progress.

Great coaching gets them there, and it comes in two different forms:

In-training... like in a training or onboarding session
In-the-moment... in real-time, as they're doing something that needs refinement or correction

Whenever you're teaching new skills or concepts to your team, wear your coach's hat. Think of a football coach on the sidelines. He can't go out there to run the plays himself, even though he knows how to win it better than anyone else on the field (sound familiar?). He can't play the game *for* them. Instead, he has to get *his players and their skills to greatness* with his coaching. The faster he can get them there, the better. Just like you.

Making sure they learn quickly is tricky. The last time you taught someone a skill set did they get it down for good the first time? Probably not. Let's make sure the things you teach stick. The first time.

In studying, tweaking and mastering great teaching[1] over decades... yes, there's an art to it. But there's also a formula. The greatest teachers and coaches useit, consciously or not. You're about to learn how to do it consciously, setting them up to win every time.

Here's an acronym to keep in mind as we break down the magic of getting it to stick...

HOW
EVERY
COACH
SUCCEEDS
CONSISTENTLY

H = Hook

Most people start with "Here's what I'm going to teach you." While that does give direction, it also blows the punchline. No matter how great your coaching is, if they don't like the punchline, they're not going to stick around for the rest. No decent comedian would start off with "Here's where I'm going with this next joke."

Instead, tell them the WIIFM. What do they really want to be able to do? To get people psyched to learn what you have to teach, start with what they will get out of it.
"Do you want to have a six pack and look great in a bathing suit by summer?" (*yes!*)

VS.

"I'm going to show you an intense abdominal workout with proper form." *(yawn)*

Get their attention by speaking to their need, their want, their issue.

If you don't start with what's in it for them, you may as well be talking to the wall. Based on my observations, I'd bet that a lot of the time you spend re-teaching is because the first time you didn't have their full attention hooked in the first place. We know that learning is State-dependent, right? So, if they're in a *distracted* state, how much are they learning? So, don't waste your time or theirs. Get them hooked first.

H - Hook:
Answering their WIIFM to get into their world
Give them a reason to say "I'm in!!!"

"What if you could...?"
"Imagine..."
"Would you be interested in..."

In-Training:
Tell them what they'll be able to master, solve or take on by the end of the training. "What if you could...?"
In-the-Moment:
Tell them what the opportunity for mastery is, and get them fired up about it. "What if you could've made those last three shots?"

Think of the last coaching moment you had, teaching a new skill, rollout, procedure, policy for something—the last moment that you were actually giving some kind of instructional coaching to somebody. Did you have a hook at the beginning? Anywhere in there? How could you have started it off with a hook? What kind of question could you have asked? What kind of "Imagine if you could..." statement could you have started with? How could you have entered their world, tapped their WIIFM a little before you got into what you were teaching them?

E = Experience

This is where you *throw them into it.*
Before you've explained exactly what and how they should do it with all the steps laid out?
Exactly!

This approach is counter to how most of us were taught, yet exactly how we actually learn in real life.
You get into a situation or experience, then form questions you need answers to in order to master or figure out what you're doing, right? That's when you learn the fastest—powered by your own need to know, understand or be able to do something.

Unfortunately real schooling:

When you were a kid in school, learning a unit about animals, when during that unit did you go on the field trip to the zoo? If you went at all, it was probably at the end of the unit- if you were good, if you got everything else covered, etc. Except which part did you remember more vividly- the chapters and textbook in the weeks before the field trip OR the actual field trip? The field trip, of course! This is backwards, yet how most of us were taught- content (coaching), then maybe an experience afterward.

How it could've gone learning:

Start off with the Experience first- the field trip to the zoo. The whole time, the teacher asks you questions like, "Do you smell that crazy bear smell? I wonder what that's about?" "Check out that color of the flamingos. Why do you think they have that?" Then, afterward the content has something to stick to back in the classroom... "Remember that bear smell?" "Yeah- that was gross! Why do they smell like that?" "Turn to page 32 of your books..." where they see the correlation between the bear's diet and his food. A-ha moment! Cool! Learning they'll never forget and were excited to learn!

So you give them the *experience first, then* the coaching to illuminate it and make the learning stick—an orchestrated a-ha moment. We've all had someone tell us what they thought was great advice or sage wisdom, only for it to go in one ear and out the other... then got to some other moment later in our lives when we *wished* we had listened to that person. We couldn't hear them when they told us in the first place, because their teaching had nothing to stick to yet!

E - Experience:
- Throw them into it
- Do it with them
- Role play it

"Think back
to a time when..."
"Try this..."

In-Training:
Give them a hands-on or personal reference before you explain it to
them. If I'm teaching somebody client or customer satisfaction, then
I'd have them either go to experience it themselves so we can talk
about it afterward, have them think of a personal experience they've
had themselves, or role-play it. This is the hands-on experience part.
I play the part of an angry client. Or I say, "Tell me about your worst
client interaction." Either way, I've just taken them into an experience
(real-time or remembered) to which they can react. *Their world.*

**Now everything I give them from here on out will have
something to stick to, because they're *in the experience* of it.**

*So, think for a moment about that very thing, that same experience you
thought about with the Hook. Did you create an experience? Did you role
play? Did you get the person you were teaching involved by tapping into
their VAK? Think about the experience you could have created. If you
could go back in time, how would you have created an experience to make
that teaching moment more personal?*

In-the-Moment:
Pause them mid-experience, as they're doing whatever it is that needs
improvement and coaching. For a basketball coach, my player is on the
court, doing what they do.
If it's practice, I pause them.
If it's a game, I call a time out. The power of the timeout is to give just-
in-time coaching and direction—when it will make the most difference.
What's you equivalent of that practice or the game?

C = Coach

I pull the player, and give them the key distinctions to make all the difference in what just happened in their experience—the **coaching** I want them to remember: "Here's what you were doing. Want that shot to go in next time? Adjust your form this way...." This is when you actually deliver the key learnings you want them to get.

Just like you don't want to blow the punchline before you tell the joke, the sequence of experience before the coaching is key. Most people do the coaching or "teaching" first and then introduce experience afterward. That's the field trip at the end of the unit, after the window of learning has passed.

In-Training:
This is the content you already have prepared, but were delivering cold before. So now deliver it, tagging the experience you gave them.
In-the-Moment:
Deliver the distinction, adjustment, technique that makes all the difference while they're right there in it. If that guidance had been delivered in the moment when you needed it most, it would've been an epiphany. Give just-in-time coaching, and you create a-ha moments of learning that stick.

In either setting, a few things to keep in mind about delivery: So, the way that you deliver the content is just as important as the content itself.

- **And Not BUT.** You saw this in *how to Tap Their WIIFM*, and it's critical here, too. "You know, what you did so far was really good, **but** if you tried these two things...."

Say the exact same sentence, just replace that word and it's a completely different experience for the person listening: "That one thing you did was really great, **and** if you try these two things too...." All of a sudden the person listening hears the positive and the constructive equally.

- **Opportunity vs. Problem**
  "So, here's a real problem we have..." or, "Here's a real opportunity we have..." People hear *opportunity* as something that we can move toward, keeps us moving forward vs. *problem*, which they hear as something's wrong or bad, and they go negative or defensive on you. Keep them positive.

C - Coaching:
Deliver the coaching while they're in the experience (or immediately after).
- Make it positive
- Answer the question or need created in their heads during the experience

- And vs. But
- Challenge vs. Problem
- Opportunity vs. Criticism

Go back to that coaching experience you recently had. How did the language you used impact the likelihood of it being heard? What could you have changed?

S = Send Them Back In

If our football coach on the sidelines is the kind who's consistently successful in developing players, it's because of what they do next...

What Not To Do

The coaches who don't see improvement happening very quickly make their mistake here. They pull the player out of the experience, deliver the coaching, but then *bench* that player to replace them with someone who already gets it. Then what happens to learning? It STOPS. The player who's benched never completes the learning cycle because they never get to cement the *right* way to do it into their kinesthetic memory after the coaching. The last experience (which we know trumps everything else) they have is *incorrect*, and *that's what sticks*. Even though they *heard* the coaching, they need to reprogram their *experience* of the new behavior into their brains by putting it into play. Otherwise it's a gamble, hoping they retain that instruction without application until next time when it counts.

This is why we see people who stop improving—their bosses keep giving them post-mortem "coaching"—too late to go back in and try out the new improved way or lock it into memory. So the next time they're back in the game, they do what's most comfortable and known to them —what they did *last* rather than the new way. And their progress stops, stuck on repeat.

What the Best Coaches Do
Send them *back into the game*.
Give the person you're coaching a chance to transfer whatever information you just gave them back into their world, their muscle memory, their completed learning. Let them try it out themselves *immediately*.

In-Training:
If you just did a role-play with them and then coached them through the steps, now have them try. Have them role-play back to you or practice it with somebody else.
In-the-Moment:
Have them go do it again, but with your coaching in play. Even better, give more coaching after and send them back in again—a few times, each with more refinement.

S - Send them back into the game:
Give them a chance to transfer the info to their reality right away. Like a football coach, you've just pulled your player, gone over the play, and now you're sending him back in to do it, completing his learning cycle.
• practice and report back
• set a learning goal

"Now - go try it!"

Think again about your last coaching experience. Did you give instruction that was immediately applicable or did you coach reactively to an experience that might not come up again for a long time? Did you bench the person you instructed or did you give them a high-five and send them back into the game? What could you do differently as a coach next time?

C = Celebrate

Picture yourself sitting in the stands at a professional football game. The quarterback throws the ball, and a receiver catches it. Play completed, yards gained. What happens in the stands? The crowd starts cheering and we go crazy.

Hmm. This guy is getting paid how many millions of dollars to do that job—literally catch the ball and keep it moving? So why are we making such a big deal of it? It's his *job* and there aren't even any points on the board from that catch! What would happen if nobody cheered until they actually scored? It would be completely boring, wouldn't it? And what would happen for that player and his teammates? Performance is all about State, right? It doesn't matter that it's his job; in the moment, even that pro needs to be mentally and emotionally set in order to physically perform consistently. We cheer for every completed pass because we know that it *keeps them going* and we're excited about *progress toward the win*. We celebrate every little gain because yards gained lead to points on the board, which lead to a win.

The same is true for every single person on your team. You coach them and they go for it all the way through trying out the new behavior after you sent them back into the game. Let's compare them with that professional football player. The person reporting to you is getting paid how many millions of dollars to do what you ask him to do? Hm. And we meet every little gain or step toward the win of mastery with what kind of celebration and reinforcement? Hm. *So Celebrate!* This is the number one thing I see missing in most corporate coaching situations. Celebrate what they just learned or attempted, that they took a big step just now outside their comfort zone and made progress. Do what a great coach does on the sidelines of a game—as that quarterback comes out after the play the coach gives him a big high five. They celebrate it.

C - Celebrate:
Anchor their success and learning early and often. This completes the learning, and gives them a chance to solidify it in their heads.

"Go, You!!!!"

This might be the most critical thing we can take as leaders from the world of sports. If you simply start celebrating every gain on the way to the win a little more like you do for those football players' completed passes, you'll be amazed to see how much more energy and effort your people put out, because it reinforces and sets their State in such a way that they just keep going for it. *Celebrate early and often.*

In-Training & In-the-Moment:
It can be just a simple high five. You can also yell, congratulate them, acknowledge them, give them a hug...whatever's appropriate. The key is that they get a positive, celebratory association with learning something new, so that the next time they know it's time to learn something new they don't have that dread in the pit of their stomach. They know that you as their coach are going to make it a positive experience.

The difference between a leader who *tells* and a leader who can truly *coach to teach* is profound. Set up the a-ha, and make it stick. That's how every coach succeeds consistently.

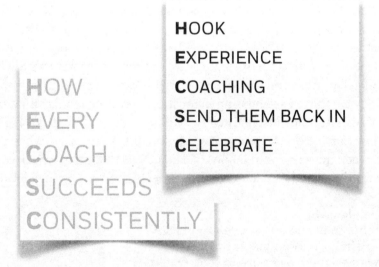

HOW
EVERY
COACH
SUCCEEDS
CONSISTENTLY

HOOK
EXPERIENCE
COACHING
SEND THEM BACK IN
CELEBRATE

Here's what this model could look, sound and feel if you tried it out.

H – Hook
Answer their WIIFM to get into their world "So, Frank, what if you had a way to get your team more bought in to what they're doing, and more responsive to your requests?" (Frank says, "That would be great – what's the catch?)

E – Experience
Give them a hands-on or personal reference before you explain it to them. "No catch – can I take part of your five-minute meeting?." (Frank agrees). You then start off the meeting in a high-energy way, and give the team feedback on some opportunities (things that they might want to try that would get them even more consistent, positive results). Because you stated them as opportunities (rather than problems or criticisms) and give them lots of positive acknowledgments with it, they are bought in, and eager to try what you've suggested. You make a date to check back with them in two days to see what's different.

C – Content
Deliver the content after they've had an experience with it. "So, Frank, what did you notice about that interaction I had with the team?" Have Frank notice the positive approach, acknowledgement, 'opportunities' instead of problems, plug for check-back, and the team's response to the positive approach. Then talk with Frank about his approach, how he can make it more positive, and the effect it'll have. Talk through how he can be more enrolling, and practice some examples.

S – Send them back into the game
Give them a chance to transfer the info to their reality right away. "OK, Frank, your turn. Now you try it out, with this person over here." You go with him as he attempts positive communication and clear requests. Then take him aside again...

C – Celebrate
Anchor their success, and learning and stepping outside their comfort zone positively. "Nicely done, Frank!" High five him, and then talk with him about the recipient's reaction, how it felt, how he can fine tune and do it more, etc.

Your Turn...

H – Hook

Answer their WIIFM to get into their world

E – Experience

Give them a hands-on or personal reference before you explain it to them.

C – Content

Deliver the content after they've had an experience with it.

S – Send them back into the game

Give them a chance to transfer the info to their reality right away.

C – Celebrate

Anchor their success, and learning and stepping outside their comfort zone positively.

Notes:

"We all know nobody's perfect, yet in those moments where that imperfection is visible to the world, all eyes and ears are on you, and how you respond sends a loud message about who you are as a person and a leader."

Chapter 15:
Above the Line

What if your team had way to communicate without any of the excuse-making, whining or complaining that you've heard in the past? Wouldn't that be great?

Completely possible. To do that, we need to talk about *The Line*.

This tool has been spread to businesses worldwide, originating[1] from some friends in the entrepreneurial personal growth world.

The Line

First, an important question: **Would you agree that no matter what you're doing orsaying at any given moment, you're sending a message to the world about who you are?** Not the entire message, but a message, nonetheless, right?

Which begs the next question: "What message am I sending?"

As a leader, your message is critical for all those reasons of magnification we know exist in your role. Your responses send messages that get blown up into characterizations about your leadership, good or bad.

Our messages when things are going well are important, yet maybe even more defining in moments when we've dropped the ball or missed the mark. We all know nobody's perfect, yet in those moments when that imperfection is visible to the world, all eyes and ears are on you, and how you respond sends a loud message about who you are as a person and a leader. You judge your team in those moments of their imperfection, and the world judges you in yours, too. *You have options.*

To illustrate how this can go, let's take a common example like meeting someone for dinner at 6:00. This could be a work person or a non-work person. You arrive at the restaurant at six, ready. You've busted your butt to get there on time, you're hungry, you're ready, you're excited. It's a crowded restaurant, a lot of people are waiting for tables, but here you are. You say, "Oh yeah, go ahead and seat us. My friend is going to be here any second."

You sit down, ready, waiting, hungry, excited. And you wait. 6:05, 6:10, 6:15. Your friend doesn't show up until 6:20, maybe even 6:25. At this point, you are irritated to say the least. They walk in. They have an opportunity in that moment. They could say any number of things, and whatever it is could either completely redeem them and make it totally okay or make things much worse, right? They've got some options...

Lay Blame

They walk in at 6:20 and they say, "Ugh! Traffic was horrible. I got caught in this accident. There was nothing I could do about it. We were sitting there and sitting there and sitting there. I couldn't move. I couldn't get past it. It was so frustrating."
Or
"You are never going to believe what happened. I was on my way out the door, and then my little girl had this big meltdown and there was nothing I could do about it, and the sitter couldn't calm her down, so I had to stay and help and...ugh! Kids, you know, what are you going to do?"
Or
"Ugh! I was on my way out of work, and at the last minute, like 10 minutes before I walked out the door, my boss dumps this project on my desk that absolutely had to get done today. They made me do it, so I had to sit there and finish it and cram to get it done and get out the door and ugh! And there you go. Here I am, twenty minutes late."

**These are all great examples of
Lay Blame.
Translation:** *It's someone or
something else's fault.*

The issue here is not whether or not that's true. Any one of those responses could be completely honest. But that doesn't matter, really. If we're always sending a message, what message is this person sending about who they are

LAY BLAME

To be clear, there are several messages we could interpret here. But we'll cut to the bad news, because that's what people will hang on to the most.

Bad news message#1: Nothing gets on me, like Teflon.
Or
Bad news message#2: I am controlled by the circumstances of my life, with no power to control it.

Either you're slippery or you're powerless. Neither is good.
Definitely not the messages you want to be sending. Especially as a leader- there's no strength there for you.

Justify
There's another way the same person could go.

They could come in and say, "Oh yeah, I know I'm 20 minutes late, but let's think about how many times you've been late."
Or
"Yeah, I'm 20 minutes late, but you never get a table right away here. I knew we'd just be waiting around standing and waiting for a table, so it's certainly not big a deal that I'm 20 minutes late."
Or
"Yeah, I'm late, but you know, it's early anyway. You know, I'm not that hungry. I knew you wouldn't be hungry either, so what's the big deal waiting a few minutes? We'll have a drink, and then we'll eat. I knew you'd just be hanging out. No problem."

These are great examples of how we Justify.
Translation = *Yes, I did that, yet here's why it's okay that I did it.*

Again—any of those things could be true, but that's not the point. You gave your word and you didn't keep it, and are justifying why. And what message does that send?

JUSTIFY
LAY BLAME

Bad news message: What I committed to wasn't that important to me, and the standard I hold myself to in keeping my word is pretty low.

Ouch. Yet as justification for your justification, this is one of the most common places below the line for leaders to come from, as there are a lot of things we're moving around for each decision, prioritizing—not everything can get first priority, so this may be the one thing that had to give. One thing over another. Yet you have the ability to respond differently.

Deny

Same scenario once again, the person walks in 20 minutes late, and they say, "All right, let's eat."

Now you're fuming at this point, right?

You say, "I'm hungry, I'm tired, I'm irritated, people are jumping all over this table. What do you mean? You're 20 minutes late. You're just going to come in here and not say anything?"

And the person offers a look of shock and says, "What? I'm not 20 minutes late. I'm actually early. We were going to meet at 6:30, not six. What are you talking about? I'm fine. Your watch must be wrong. Maybe you didn't check your calendar right. I'm definitely on time."

Hm.

That's what it sounds like to Deny.
Translation: *I didn't do it or I didn't know.*

Maybe there was truly a miscommunication. Or maybe this person is just in denial. What does it say about the you when you Deny?

DENY
JUSTIFY
LAY BLAME

Bad news message #1: I am completely out of touch with reality.
Or
Bad news message #2: I am a liar, and can't really be trusted. Neither of these is good, obviously. Zero personal power.

Quit

Once again, you're there in the restaurant. The person walks in, just throws up their hands and says, "What are you going to do? I'm just cursed to be late my entire life. I don't know what it is.
I try to be on time. I try to leave early. I try to get it—keep it together, I'm just always late. What am I going to do?"
Or
When you ask where they've been, they give you the hand, roll their eyes, and say, "Whatever." With a little attitude.
Or
They send you a text at 6:25 that only says, "Forget it—can't get there." And that's it.

These are all different forms of Quit.
Translation: *Yes, I did it, and I've given up on any chance it could go another way.*

QUIT
DENY
JUSTIFY
LAY BLAME

Perhaps there is, indeed, a pattern of failure here. Or a big challenge they keep coming up against. As a leader,

that's not uncommon. Yet when a
person responds by giving up like this, what message does it send
about who they are?

Bad news message: I don't have what it takes to stay in the game. Sort
of pathetic.

Regular Human Defaults
So, you don't want to come from any of these places. In the game of life,
we could say that all of these spots below the line put us on the Victim
team, in a pretty powerless place. And yet we do it. We go below the
line.

You go there, I go there, and so do all the people you interact with all
day. We go there because each one of those spots below the line is a
normal human defense mechanism. You probably have a default
favorite, which you find yourself doing more than the others, right?
Own it.

Then choose another way. Because now we know better, having just
shone a light on it and labeled it. And now you get the cost in what
you're unintentionally saying to the world about who we are.

Above the Line
Your friend arrives at the restaurant 20 minutes late and says, "Wow!
I just want to acknowledge that I'm 20 minutes late, that you were
probably here on time, you were sitting here probably hungry,
probably irritated. I didn't even call. And I'm sure that had more effect
on you than just wasted time. I apologize for that. What can I do to
make it right? (and you get to answer) I recommit to keeping my word
next time or if something comes up at least calling you as soon as I
know."

That's called Response-ability.
Translation: *Yes I did it. And I'm going to own it.*

Good news message: I have choices. I am a regular human being who makes mistakes, which affect other people, and I have the ability to choose my response every time to show some personal power by owning it and *making it right*.

Now, it's not that any of the other circumstantial things didn't happen. There could have been the traffic jam, there could have been the meltdown with the little girl, or the boss putting the project on the desk right as she was walking out the door, or a misunderstanding or a pattern of lateness.

Any of those things could be true, but they didn't go there.
They came from above the line. Whether you are 20 minutes late for dinner or giving the boss a project update, you have a choice in how you respond. You may not have control of the circumstances, but you have complete control of the way you respond to it.

RESPONSE-ABILITY

QUIT
DENY
JUSTIFY
LAY BLAME

It's about the relationship, not the excuse.
Trust is like the fabric that holds your relationships together. Every time I give my word and then I don't keep it, there's a little rip in that fabric with that person on the receiving end. Just like a rip in my shirtsleeve, if I don't address and fix it asap, it keeps tearing more and more. If I leave it, it'll eventually unravel completely.

As you know from your own experience, when you're on the receiving end with someone who's going below the line, it's hard to hear anything they're saying, because all you really want them to do is own it and make it right with you. Short of them having experienced bodily harm or something, you don't really care why they dropped the ball— you just want them to own it and clean it up with you. Address the rip first and repair it.

This is a deliberate choice. When you communicate from above the line, it's not about the excuse or the circumstances, it's about your word, keeping your word, maintaining your word and taking care of the relationship.

Reality

It's much easier to come from below the line than above it. I've been teaching this concept for over 20 years, and I still go below the line every day. The difference now is that it rarely comes out of my mouth anymore. I'm proud to report that I now catch myself first, remind myself that I have the ability to respond differently, and do.

But we get sucked under the line because *it's what we do as humans.* Our brains go there naturally, our little voice steers us there, and we can even get people to support us there. People especially love to jump on the blame or justify wagons with you, to make you feel better, often in the name of justice or what's "right" ("You shouldn't have been penalized for that—everyone else is doing it, too! Especially him...."). You even know people right now who live their whole lives below the line, right? And you've definitely seen leaders who operate from there. Sketchy.

So it's a choice. Not the natural or easy one, yet the one that gives you so much more freedom. Once you call it, own it, and move on...you're done. It's over. The trust is repaired, you don't have to carry around your guilt anymore and you are free to move about your life. Below the line, it's messy, and there's always residue in your head, the relationship and your conscience. And you don't have time for carrying around extra residue in your head, right?

Possible Reality

What would happen if everyone on your team started communicating from only above the line? What would happen? Dynamics and communication might look, sound and feel really different, wouldn't they? How about in your family? In society?

I can't speak for society, but I can attest that there are many companies I've worked with where after introducing Above the Line, it has become standard vocabulary and a pillar of their cultures. In the middle of a meeting, somebody might hold up a little hand signal to a teammate of "This is the line," and then with their other hand point to a place below it, signaling "Hello, you're below the line. Rewind, try that again." And they call each other out using language like that supports each to come back up above the line if someone falls below it.

Call it. Own it. Move on.

The key here is *not* making a mandate to say "Nobody may ever come from below the line again." That would be a set up for failure (see the "Reality" section a few pages ago), because we're all regular human beings and we all do it—we're just supporting one another to choose another way to communicate that's cleaner. There's no busting people below the line—just a kind-yet-direct calling-out of it, to bring it to someone's awareness as they do it unconsciously. People say, "Oh, you're right. I was below the line. Let me try that again." Then they own it, fix it and move on. It's a beautiful thing.

Leaders tell me that once their people get this idea and start using it with one another, morale goes up, the way people communicate gets clearer, backbiting against one another internally goes down. Instead, they start supporting one another, and a lot of the complaining, drama and whining typical in work cultures just goes away. It can shift the whole dynamic of how your people communicate with one another and with you.

Before you consider introducing an idea like this into your team, try it on yourself. For a *while*.

Start to notice where you're coming from yourself--above or below the line. When you *do* go below the line, which is your default? What triggers it for you? Maybe certain topics trigger Deny for you, while certain people bring out the Lay Blame in you. Catch yourself out loud, so people can see you self-correcting. The more you do this, the more you're modeling the behavior you want them to try while you're re-training your own reactions. Quickly, you'll get to the point of catching yourself before you go below the line, and get yourself up above it out loud.

> **Introducing it to the team:**
> For every team I lead, I practice Above the Line response-ability myself, then introduce it to the team by explaining it as something I'm working on and asking for their support on in helping me stay above the line. "This is something I'd love your support with. Would you point it out when you notice me going below the line?" Of course they agree- who doesn't want to call their boss out? Then I say, "And can I return that favor? Can we support one another in trying this out?" They agree, because I stepped out of my comfort zone as a leader admitting my own so-human tendencies first, making it safe for them and establishing credibility myself.

As a leader, your responses send messages about who you are, which get magnified by your position. Tiny rips in that fabric of trust can quickly unravel your credibility and integrity in their eyes when you slip below the line.

Call it. Own it. Move on, *above* the line.

Notes:

I mean it.
sarah@sarahsingerandco.com

Chapter 16:
The Beginning

Are you full yet?

We've covered a lot so far in these pages—more than most people in leadership positions ever consider. Yet now you're thinking about it with specificity and depth. You now have a different level of consciousness about yourself and your options as a leader than you did at the beginning of this book. One leader described that sensation to me this way: "It's like I'm looking at myself through a rear-view mirror —from a different vantage point outside myself, seeing things I just couldn't see before." That self-awareness is a great thing, yet a little unsettling because you're still in that sweet spot of learning, vacillating between "Doh—there I go again with the 2 over their head" and "Hey, I've got this!"

We're Just Getting Started.

This is not a read-and-shelve book. Once you finish this last chapter, the best part of the process *begins*! This book is meant to become your manual and guidebook as you transfer every idea in here smoothly into your practice as a leader.

To do that, give yourself some space and process to make it happen. If you just read through in a straight shot, go back now and start to really dig in; try the tools, layer by layer, in your own world.

You'll know when you *really get* each tool or framework, because you'll distinctly feel, see or hear a shift. Something opens up where it was closed before, something accelerates that was stuck before, something surfaces that you couldn't see before, something connects that was distant before, someone gets it who couldn't before, someone expands, who was limited before...because *you're* tapping into something you didn't before.

So here's the most important part after 15 chapters and tools:

What have you learned?

What surprised you about yourself?

What challenged you?
What validated you?
What did you rethink?
Who did you reconsider?
What have you tapped into as a leader?

I said at the beginning that this process wasn't about managing. Of course a lot needs to be managed in your world—in the work, the details, the plans, the organization of things. Yet now you know that being the leader who taps into greatness creates impact so much bigger than one tryng to manage it all. You now know how to make a difference in the lives of everyone you touch.

It's easy to think of leadership as a mysterious gift that someone either innately gets, or they don't. Now you know that it's not quite as simple as that, right? Being the leader who elevates the game, drives the biggest impact and taps greatness all around you is doable, learnable and purposeful. It's also a *practice*.

You are a leader, evolving. You always have been, and now your evolution is accelerating with new self-awareness and a shiny new set of tools to learn how to use deftly, intentionally, impactfully. As you get more and more comfortable with these tools, tapping people's greatness will become more of the new standard you set for yourself than the surprise that happens in a great moment. You'll be able to do it any time, any place, with any kind of personality.

This approach will go from ideas you once read in a book...to how you lead.

Here's How:

Lock it In.
Remember at the halfway point, when we stopped, assessed what we'd done so far and got really clear about it to make sure all of those pieces were rock solid before we added the second half? Do that now with the second half or the whole thing. Remember—10-24-7 to get it in there all

the way? Reflect on each of the chapters, using your VAK.

- **Visual:** read the notes you made and write new ones. Sketch images. Create sticky-note reminders. Notice responses in your people as you expand their game.
- **Auditory:** Talk about the ideas. Share them with your colleagues. Talk through what they mean to you and how you want to implement them. Talk to your little voice, and get it on your side.
- **Kinesthetic:** Play with the concepts, test them through the muscle memory of real life, and practice them. Pay attention to how they feel different from your normal approach, and allow yourself to get comfortable with them—each piece you have gone through, learned, tried out in your own world and now are honing and tweaking and perfecting on your way to mastery as you added these pieces into your repertoire as a leader.

Take it in layers.
Every tool or idea in this book works best when layered with the others. You can use many simultaneously, and will. As you're learning them, however, break them down. I suggest taking them one week at a time, so you can really focus in on them in practice. As you do...

Chart your progress.
Remember that one of our Big 3 motivators is Mastery.
Seeing that we're making progress is important. Yet seeing HOW you're making progress is golden. So chart it. Maybe by week (here's what I tried this week), by tool (here's where I am with this one), by layer (here's what distinctions I'm adding now). Whatever works best for how you learn. As you do, track a few elements for each piece:

- **Ease.** What did you try, how did it feel, and how was it smoother than last time?
- **Response.** How did it go? What was the response? What ripple effect did it have?
- **WIIFM.** What did you gain out of doing it? What did it open up, shift or cause in its impact?
- **Tweaks.** What do you want to change or adjust the next time you try it?

Use a cheat sheet.
It seems that the moment you need a tool the most is the same moment
you can't remember it, right? So, it's great to have a reference to jog
your memory and get you right on the path. Create a list of the
concepts plus the passages that stood out to you. Make that into a cue
card you can carry with you, glance at when needed, or review on a
plane or in the car. I've had many people reduce one of those lists down
to pocket size or wallet size, laminate them and carry them around
with them always as a great reference tool.[1]

It's coming through.
Your team will notice a difference in you as you practice these tools.
Maybe they already have noticed, if you've taken some time to read
and implement as you've gone. You've changed your thinking in many
ways. You're accessing states that you weren't accessing before. You're
tapping greatness in them that you weren't before. With hope, they've
noticed these changes. And there's only one way to find out...

Ask them for feedback.
Have they noticed anything? If they say no, that's going to be a great
big red flag for you. If they say yes, ask them for details. I find that the
more you ask for feedback from people, the more honest they'll get.
If you've never asked them for feedback before, they might be a little
taken aback by it and they might tell you exactly what you want to hear
at first. Yet if you ask them on a regular basis for feedback, they'll give
you more and more detail.

Reach out.
Feel free to reach out anytime if there's a question you have
along the way, or you've got a great example of something you tried
that worked wonders to share. I mean it.
sarah@sarahsingerandco.com

Finally...thank you so much. Thank you for the time and attention
you've invested in this process. Most importantly, thank you for the
personal investment you've made in what's possible not just for your
people, but for you too.

Greatness has been in there the whole time. You knew that before you ever read this book, or you wouldn't have opened it in the first place. Now you can see it, access it, and choose to pull it up and out in 15+ different ways for yourself and everyone around you into huge impact. That's the difference between a great manager and a phenomenal leader. That's what Tapping Into Greatness is all about.

It's all you.
Trust yourself, believe in them and you will tap greatness every time. You've got this. And I'm behind you, committed to your success 100%!

GO!!!!

Notes:

Chapter Resources

Chapter 0: Let's Go!

1. All the distinctions and tools in this book can be used as team and cultural tools, and I often coach them that way in my work with organizations. When everyone on a team uses these with one another, their collective impact jumps to another level. That said, this book focuses in on you as the leader, and how to tap everyone else's greatness as you lead. The more you practice the tools here, the more your people will notice, and the dynamic on your team will change as a result.

2. While I continue to study the works of many from afar, I've had the great opportunity to learn directly from Blair Singer, Mark Reardon, Bobbi DePorter, Eric Jensen, Jayne Johnson, Ceil Stanford, Robert Kiyosaki, Harv Ekert, Linda Brown, Rich Allen, Tony Robbins and the awesome leaders at The Landmark Forum.

3. *www.sarahsingerandco.com*

4. A quick head's up here. You might think you're the type of person who learns motionlessly. But understand that there's more research than I can cite here to prove that kinesthetic (involving motion and emotion) learning sticks way faster and longer than any other mode. So, as we continue on through the book, there will be times that I ask you to do things that may seem a little strange or awkward. Do it anyhow, and watch how you retain the information so easily.

Chapter 1: The Third Who

1. The idea of a little voice in your head is pervasive, because it's real for every human on the planet. The master trainer of little voice is Blair Singer, who's created a whole lineup of *Little Voice Mastery*™ support for you, including the book, audio programs and powerful coaching support in the *Little Voice Mastery*™*Mentoring Program!*
• Singer, Blair. *Little Voice Mastery: How to Win the War between Your Ears in 30 Seconds or Less and Have an Extraordinary Life!* New York: Select, 2011.
• www.blairsinger.com/little-voice-mastery

2. Seligman created this frame over years with his own research team and Dr. John Teasdale, building on the work of attribution theory (Bernard Weiner)

3. Seligman, Martin. *Learned Optimism: How To Change Your Mind and Your Life.* New York: Pocket Books, 1990.

4. Seligman created this frame over years with his own research team and Dr. John Teasdale, building on the work of attribution theory (Bernard Weiner).

5. You could spend years tinkering with the nuanced study of reading their signs in facial expression, body language and eye movements. We'll cover some good basics in Chapter #10: VAK

Chapter 2: WIIFM

1. WIIFM is an idea that has made its way into mainstream language. Unfortunately, it's usually used as an ironic cliche, as in "Isn't she just tuned into one radio station only- WIIFM?" In this conversation, we're not joking about it or seeing it as a bad thing at all. It's human motivation.

2. Pink, Daniel H. *Drive: The Surprising Truth about What Motivates Us.* New York, NY: River-head, 2009.

Chapter 3: Your Process

1. Commonly referred to as the *Conscious-Competence Learning Model* this framework's origin is hard to pinpoint. While Maslow, Socrates and Confucius all have writings similar, the 4-stage model itself is most notably sourced to Martin Broadwell in 1969 or Noel Burch (Gordon Training

International) in 1970.

2 .You may be wondering why I'm asking you to draw and write this out if it's already printed on these pages? Because the act of writing it yourself as you learn it will ensure that it sticks in your memory and has more meaning way faster and longer than if you just see it printed on these pages. Do this throughout the book, anytime I introduce a diagram of any kind, or you visualize one in your mind as you're reading. I'm all about you learning, not just reading this, my friend.

3. The term "downshifting"has been both widely used and hotly debated through the worlds of neuroscience and its application into education and mainstream. It references the idea of "triune brain,"from Dr. Paul Maclean(1970), former chief of the Laboratory of Brain Evolution and Behavior of the National Institute of Mental Health. Triune brain was Maclean's way to explain different systems (most notably the limbic system) in the brain responsible for some human responses we had yet to understand. Our understanding of how neural activity occurs in the brain has evolved quite a bit since Maclean's theory was introduced, yet downshifting is still referenced as a great metaphor to understand the sudden shift in our thinking and reactive capacity.

4. "Emotional hijacking"is another term to describe what happens in those fight or flight moments, coined by Dr. Daniel Goleman in Emotional Intelligence, a must-read.

• Goleman, Daniel. *Emotional Intelligence*. New York: Bantam, 1995. Print.
• Maclean, Paul. *The Truine Brain in Evolution: Role in Paleocerebral Functions*. Springer. 1990. Print.
• LeDoux, Joseph E. *The Emotional Brain: The Mysterious Underpinnings of Emotional Life*. New York: Simon & Schuster, 1996. Print.
• Pert, Candace B. *Molecules of Emotion: Why You Feel the Way You Feel*. New York, NY: Scribner, 1997. Print.
• Sylwester, Robert. "The Downshifting Dilemma: A Commentary and Proposal" *New Horizons in Learning, School of Education*, Johns Hopkins University, October, 1998.

5. Positive doesn't mean pressure-free. There can be high stakes and high pressure in the game without downshifting. Threat is the key trigger to avoid.

6. The talent question is a big one. Learnable or not? My favorite sources on this topic are:

• Buckingham, Marcus, and Donald O. Clifton. *Now, Discover Your Strengths*. New York: Free, 2001. Print.
• Buckingham, Marcus and Clifton, Donald. *Now Discover Your Strengths*. New York: The Free Press. 2001. Print.
• Coyle, Daniel. *The Talent Code: Greatness Isn't Born: It's Grown, Here's How*. New York: Bantam, 2009. Print.
• Dweck, Carol. *Mindset*, New York: Random House. 2006. Print.
• Gladwell, Malcolm. Outliers. *New York: Little Brown and Company*. 2007. Print.

7. Most notably...

• Clifton, Donald and Nelson, Paula. *Soar With Your Strengths*. New York: Dell Publishing. 1996. Print.
• Robinson, Ken. *Finding Your Element: How Finding Your Passion Changes Everything*. New York: Penguin Books. 2009. Print.

9. Check out the Clifton StrengthFinder. It's brilliant, and will change the way your team defines its strengths. Go to www.gallupstrengthscenter.com, where you can download the diagnostic for you and your whole team. You can also get access to it with its full-book guide (my preference) in any of these books (they all give you access to the same diagnostic):

• Buckingham, Marcus and Clifton, Donald O. (2001) Now, Discover Your Strengths. New York: The Free Press. Print.
• Rath, Tom. Strengthsfinder 2.0 New York: GallupPress. 2007. Print.

• Conchie, Barry and Rath, Tom. *Strengths-Based Leadership*. New York: GallupPress. 2008.

Chapter 4: Your Options

1. Wiseman, Liz. *Multipliers: How the Best Leaders Make Everyone Smarter*. New York: Harper Collins. 2010. Print.

Chapter 5: Impact Is ALL YOU

1. Bucky Fuller taught us precessional effect: that much of the impact of our actions occurs ninety degrees away from where we're focused. Drop a stone to get to the bottom of a pond, and the ripples it causes on the water cause impact on the pond's edge- 90 degrees away from the direction of the stone's travel.

• Edmondson, Amy. *A Fuller Explanation: The Synergetic Geometry of R. Buckminster Fuller*. New York: Emergent World LLC. 2009.

• Fuller, R. Buckminster. *Critical Path. 2nd Edition*. New York: St. Martin's Griffin.1982.

Chapter 6: Setting Yourself Up

1. The best coaches call timeouts when the stakes are highest and they need to reset things quickly. Do that for yourself when you know your BE isn't right.

2. One of my best coaches is my husband Colin. He watched me TRY to be a runner for years, making excuses, justifying reasons and complications, getting in my own way. One day he finally said, "If you're going to be a runner, then just be a runner. Runners run." And he pushed me out of our apartment (literally) and locked the door until I just ran. I've been a runner ever since.

Chapter 7: Coaching Impact

1. This coaching model was first created as Results Coaching, an adaptation of Blair Singer's Results Model, which opened up the way leaders were able to understand their results as something that started way before their plan. The original model was:

> Belief/Conditioning -> Attitude/Mindset -> Behavior -> Result, yet has evolved into
> Self-Concept -> Attitude/Mindset -> Behavior -> Result

• Singer, Blair. *Team Code of Honor: The Secrets of Champions in Business and in Life (Rich Dad's Advisors)* Paradise Valley, AZ: RDA Press, LLC. 2012.

Chapter 8: Playing Bigger

1. Watch for downshifting here. When some people are really confronted by stepping outside their comfort zone, they actually get super tired; their brain wants to go unconscious, like they can't handle staying awake for it. It's just another form of shutting down.

2. You know how to do this now from Chapter #6, right? Who do you tend to be about stepping out? Who do you need to be instead? What can you setup for yourself so you stay/get into the version of your self you need to BE to step out?

3. Dweck, Carol. *Mindset*, New York: Random House. 2006.

4. Seligman, Martin. *Learned Optimism: How to Change your Mind and Your Life*. New York: Pocket Books. 1991.

6. Brené Brown: *The Biggest Myth About Vulnerability* | Inc. Magazine video: https://www.youtube.com/watch?v=ZkDaKKkFi6Y

Also check out any Brene's Brown's TED Talks, books and articles/

• Brown, Brene. *Daring Greatly: How the Courage to Be Vulnerable Transforms the Way We Live, Love, Parent, and Lead*. New York: Gotham Books. 2012.

Chapter 9: State

1. Watch the 2004 Olympics Mens Gymnastics finals, an unbelievable display of one champion's state getting thrown, and every other competitor losing theirs too.

2. Fredrickson, Barbara. *Positivity: Top-Notch Research Reveals the 3 to 1 Ratio That Will Change Your Life*. New York: Harmony. 2009.

3. Covey, Stephen R. *The 7 Habits of Highly Effective People: Powerful Lessons in Personal Change*. New York: Free Press. 2004.

4. Genie LaBorde. *Influencing With Integrity*. Mountain View: Syntony Publishing. 1987.

Chapter 10: VAK

1. Supercamp was that transformative program. Go to www.supercamp.com.

2. The concept of Visual, Auditory Kinesthetic Modalities originates from the pioneering work of NLP: Neuro Linguistic Programming, developed by Richard Bandler and John Grinder in the 1970s. NLP focuses on understanding and working with our unconscious patterns (programming) of language (linguistic) and thinking (neuro). According to Grinder's description in his Foreword to *Influencing With Integrity*, VAK is an example of "a series of models of human excellence with special emphasis on patterns of communication. We uncovered ways to recognize and codify the specific skills by which excellent communicators achieve their outcomes.... the result of NLP, but not NLP itself." VAK has made its way into the mainstream, mostly in the world of education and learning. Its power as we work with it here is in the way you can use it to communicate more powerfully. Here are a few more resources to take it further:

• Genie LaBorde. *Influencing With Integrity*. Mountain View: Syntony Publishing. 1987. Print.

• Miles, Elizabeth. *Tune Your Brain: Using Music to Manage Your Mind, Body and Mood*. New York: Berkley Books. 1997.

• Markova, Dawna. *The Open Mind: Exploring the 6 Patterns of Natural Intelligence*. Boston, MA: Conari Press, 1996.

• Grinder, Michael. *Righting the Educational Conveyor Belt*. Portland: Metamorphous Press, 1991.

3. Most of us take notes and notes during meetings as we were taught to do in school ("must write it or you won't remember it"), even though we look at them days later and remember very little. Read *Quantum Teaching* or Bobbi DePorter's *Quantum Learning* for more ideas on VAK and how to take memorable notes in a way your brain actually stores information visually. To see research and examples of visual notes only...

• Buzan, Tony. *The MindMap Book*. London: BBC Books. 1993.

4. If someone is missing one of the three modalities, we usually refer to it as a disability- like deafness, blindness or being physically paralyzed. More research is coming online all the time to show that these modalities can still be very active in the brain even when the body can't co-operate to access them. For our purposes here, I've written the rest of this chapter to apply to guide you with folks who have access to all three modalities.

5. Sylwester, Robert."*How Emotions Effect Learning*," Educational Leadership, ASCD. 1994; and a few other great sources for emotions in learning and memory:

• Damasio, Antonio. *The Feeling of What Happens: Body and Emotion in the Making of Conciousness*. New York: Harcourt. 1999.

• Diamond, Marian and Hopson, Janet. *Magic Trees of the Mind: How to Nurture Your Child's Intelligence, Creativity, and Healthy Emotions from Birth Through Adolescence*. New York: Dutton. 1998.

• Jensen, Eric. *The Learning Brain*. San Diego, CA: Turning Point, 1994.

• Jensen, Eric, and Eric Jensen. *Brain-based Learning: The New Paradigm of Teaching*. Thousand Oaks, CA.: Corwin, 2008.

• LeDoux, Joseph. *The Emotional Brain: The Mysterious Underpinnings of Emotional Life*. New York: Simon & Schuster. 1996.

6. Studies show that intensely negative emotional experiences can get blocked in permanent memory. Don't intentionally go there.

7. This is why we see kids fall out of the educational system, most at-risk learners being super kinesthetic. If they're not engaged and don't get to move around (which gets worse as they get into higher grades) and they feel like a teacher doesn't like them...they stop trying, and ultimately take themselves out of the game. A disproportionate number of dropouts are kinesthetic learners. My favorite resource for parents and teachers, which addresses this head-on with practical how-to instruction for VAK learners: Michael Grinder's *Righting the Educational Conveyor Belt*.

Chapter 11: In-10-tion

1. I first wrote about this idea with Mark Reardon and Bobbi DePorter in our co-authored book, *Quantum Teaching: Orchestrating Student Success* (1998). They continue to demonstrate and teach its power with learners and teachers through Supercamp and Quantum Learning programs.

2. This is the learned helplessness that Martin Seligman writes about. It's a result of their conditioning over time and their explanatory style discussed in Chapter #1.

3. Psychologist Albert Bandura as has examined how we define our own capacity in terms of self-efficacy. While our own past performance shows up as a big contributor to the number we hold over our own heads. Bandura isolated past performance, vicarious experience, verbal persuasion, and emotional cues as the big four sources of self-efficacy, how I feel about my own capacity.

• Bandura, A. "Self-efficacy mechanism in human agency."American Psychologist, 37, 122-147. 1982

4. Rosenthal's original study was done in 1968, illustrated in:

• Rosenthal, R., and Jacobson, L. (1992), *Pygmalion in the Classroom*. New York: Irvington.
Yet, 30 years later Rosenthal has been validated through over 345 separate studies on this effect by diverse researchers across 8 domains including education, workplace, sports and law. His compilation is best summarized in:

• Rosenthal, Robert. "*Interpersonal Expectancy Effects: A 30-Year Perspective*." Journal of the American Psychological Society. Volume 3, Number 6, December 1994. Cambridge University Press.

5. There are people who react in an opposite way with their performance. I'm that way. If someone believes I can't it makes me want to do it and crush it even more, firing me up to prove them wrong.

6. Fredrickson, Barbara. *Positivity: Top-Notch Research Reveals the 3 to 1 Ratio That Will Change Your Life*. New York: Crown. 2009.

Chapter 12: The Three Ingredients

1. One of the most important leadership books you can have on your shelf:

• Buckingham, Marcus, and Curt Coffman. *First, Break All the Rules: What the World's Greatest Managers Do Differently*. New York, NY.: Simon & Schuster, 1999.

2. Take Dan Pink's introvert-extrovert test to see where you fall on the spectrum: http://www.danpink.com/assessment

3. Pink, Daniel H. *To Sell Is Human: The Surprising Truth about Moving Others*. New York: Riverhead, 2012.

4. Don't get me started on Machiavellian management. And please don't practice it.

5. Kohn, Alfie. *Punished by Rewards: The Trouble with Gold Stars, Incentive Plans, A's, Praise, and Other Bribes*. Boston: Houghton Mifflin, 1993. Print. Pink, Daniel H. *Drive: The Surprising Truth about What Motivates Us*. New York, NY: Riverhead, 2009.

Chapter 13: The Pyramid of Perspective

1. The origin of this idea was developed one 1980's summer with collaborators Eric Jensen and Whitney Callender, as we searched for the ultimate way to help the team of hotshot leaders we were training and leading keep perspective as they got pushed with the stress of leading intense programs back to back for weeks. Since then, I've evolved into a tool that's brought calm and depth to decisions, leaders and processes across many industries.

2. Schwartz, Tony, Jean Gomes, Catherine McCarthy. *The Way We're Working Isn't Working: The Four Forgotten Needs That Energize Great Performance*. New York: Free, 2011. Print. This is one of the most important reads for you as a leader on the implications of how we spend our energy, and how to best pulse for maximum efficiency in the face of the our society's in-creasing pace. Schwartz's team at The Energy Project bring clarity and inspired ways to work smarter- check them out!

3. Unless you tell them Why, people make up their own reasons to explain Why things are happening or Why you're deciding what you are as their leader...and they're almost always negative. The "need to know"approach for sharing why things are happening (especially in tenuous situations) usually causes unnecessary drama as people fill in the gaps with worst-case scenarios. Just tell them, so everyone's working with the same orientation.

4. Pink, Daniel H. *Drive: The Surprising Truth about What Motivates Us*. New York, NY: Riverhead, 2009.

5. *Five Whys* is helpful in many conversations- not just getting to your biggest Why. As you and your team are exploring an idea or initiative, it's easy to get excited or bogged down by the When, How, and What of it. Pause at any moment to take the group through 5 layers of Why are we doing this? until you can illuminate the biggest game for everyone.

6. Sinek, Simon. *Start with Why: How Great Leaders Inspire Everyone to Take Action*. New York: Portfolio, 2009.

Chapter 14: Making It Stick

1. This coaching frame is based on the Quantum Teaching design frame for teachers, which has transformed the way teachers approach their content all over the world. Since then, I've built HECSC out of it, and tested it as a coaching tool in retail, hospitality, financial services. For all the nuance of becoming a master teacher, check out my book *Quantum Teaching: Orchestrating Student Success*, where Bobbi Deporter, Mark Reardon and I break it down for you in vivid detail.

• DePorter, Bobbi, Mark Reardon, and Sarah Singer-Nourie. *Quantum Teaching: Orchestrating Student Success*. Boston, MA: Allyn and Bacon, 1999. Print.

2. Another gem from Quantum Teaching!

Chapter 15: Above the Line

1. Above the Line was first developed in a program called Money and You as a tool for entrepreneurs. It's shifted the way people communicate in businesses, schools, and lives all over the world. www.moneyandyou.com

A Bit About Me

1. Supercamp programs are still changing kids lives for the better all over the world for middle school, high school and college- aged youth. If you have or know kids, give them the gift of this program's im-pact simply unmatched anywhere else.

www.supercamp.com 1-800-28LEARN

3. Eric Jensen and Bobbi Deporter, founders.

Acknowledgements

I am deeply grateful for the following critically awesome people, without whom this book could not have happened...

First and foremost, Colin Nourie, my partner, love, most trusted strategic advisor, husband and best friend, for whom I am inarticulately grateful every single day. His willingness to carry way more than his part of our 3-kid, 2-business, multi-project lives, in order for for me to disappear into this writing (and other consuming sprints) is beyond reasonable, especially while also launching his own beautiful new work and design into the world. Super-dad and super-husband *almost* capture his status. Almost.

Rae, Zoe and Micah, for the light they create in the world every day as amazing human beings. Their flexibility and support of what I do inspires me as I do it, even when it takes me away from home.

My parents, whose unyielding belief in me created space for possibility. They listened to my ideas, indulged my questions, and encouraged my ventures, proudly backing my vision on every front. My siblings Blair, Tim and Betsy, whose solidly loving presence my entire life support me as I learn loudly and sometimes messily through growth.

Two educators who made all the difference— Dr. Paul Wachtel, who saw past my attitude as a high school student and gave me an opening to shine, and Joann Evans, who had a vision of what was possible and took a chance on me as young teacher committed to doing it differently.

The book team who came together to make this project happen on a ridiculously short timeline:
• Content editor and driver Craig Heimbuch, the great brain-picker and fellow author who enthusiastically sifted through and translated reams of transcription and hours of audio into real prose for me to build on; collaborated versions of possibility, then smoothed out my writing in the end. He kept me producing and actively fighting the resistance all writers face with positivity. And he enrolled, then led the uber team* to create the final pages you're flipping right now:

• Copy editor Jack Heffron*, whose ease, exactness and on-itness as a well-published author and editor himself made the reading of this book easier for you.
• Interior graphic designer Jared Fite*, who flexibly and beautifully created every page, adjusting and tweaking all the way through sunrise the very last night with me until print deadline.
• Identity and cover designer Jesse Reed, whose talent and ability to visually translate my energy never fails (check out jessereedfromohio.com)
• Publishing guru and partner Mona Gambetta, who guided me all the way through to the foil imprint.
• The RDA Press team, who took on this new title and imprint to get *Tap Into Greatness* into the world.

Clutch Advisor-Friends-With-Awesome-Talent:
• Brandon Sosna, whose critical first reads and awesome feedback of my drafts zoomed in to pinpoint what was working or missing in my writing, whose questions made me and rewrite and rethink with more clarity and whose ideas improved the reading experience of this book.
• Dev Patnaik, whose talent and support landed exactly when I needed it most, un-coincidentally including downtown Minneapolis, just in time.
• Gil Kaufman, who patiently coached, and will ultimately chip the jargon out of my sentences.
• Chris Evans, who ever-generously shared his talented team and valuable insights.

I am so grateful for the opportunity to make a difference in the world through my work, and watch it shift people's lives. The magnitude of that isn't lost on me. I've been honored to coach so many game-changing leaders, and am humbled by how they've championed my work, bringing it with them as they take on new horizons and levels of impact. Each of the following have become trusted partners and likeminded friends in the business of changing the game from the inside out, by changing the way people tap into greatness:
Udaya Patnaik, Julie Beckman, John Wiley, Joe Kerin, Joe Baron, Adam Miller, Joe Hash, Gail Taggart, Carey Cooper, Patrick Douglas

...and Darren Mangus, who kicked this book into high gear.

A Bit About Me

I present as mischievous or disruptive, yet what's really going on under that is insatiable curiosity, a lot of impatience on my way to taking action and dogged belief in possibility.

As a kid I loved to learn, inserted myself into adult conversations with strong viewpoints of my own and read way before I was supposed to (usually way past my bedtime with a flashlight under my covers). So, you would think I'd be a great learner and love school, right? Wrong.

I liked it in the beginning, but as the grades progressed, it seemed to be less about discovery or real learning and more about random information to regurgitate or perform in some other form. I started becoming an impatiently disgruntled student. By fifth grade I was the kid in class with the attitude. To me, real learning was discovering things and ideas so that we could create new ones. Or testing ideas to see what we could find out about them. But school felt confining—being told what to do and how to do it, skipping the Whys, sitting in my chair all day without even talking unless someone called on me. That seemed arbitrary and silly to me, and was not anything I wanted to be a part of or go along with, although everyone else was.

My unrefined little voice wasn't very quiet or contained to my head. It came out of my mouth all the time, which caused problems. I asked teachers, 'Why do we need to do it like that?' and 'What's the point of doing this assignment?' and my teachers weren't so interested in having those conversations with me over and over about everything they taught, as you might imagine. So, I spent a lot of time in the counselor's office, in the principal's office or with my parents in conferences debating with adults about the Why of it...and no one could really come up with a very compelling reason to me, of why I should do what they asked me to do.

By the time I got to high school, I was pretty surly about it, and pretty disenchanted with the whole process of school. I didn't care about grades—no motivation to get a grade just so I could move on to the next class, which seemed like more of the same. So I found my meaning and my niche other ways—performing or leading nonacademic initiatives in the school, or exploring thoughts in creative writing classes, and was maddening in all of my core classes. I engaged and got As with the few teachers who made it relevant to me, and I blew off the rest. I had a label stamped on my file in the counselor's office, and what felt like my forehead too, all the time: "GIFTED UNDERACHIEVER." I was lectured, "Well, it's not that you can't do it. You can. You're not just applying yourself." And I would say, "Yeah. And tell me why I should." They couldn't.

Then, at 15, the course of my life changed. My brother Blair, who notoriously knows when to reach into my life at different points, calling out what needs to shift, and urge me to the right place just in time before I implode,[1] got me to go to a 10-day summer program some of his friends had started, called SuperCamp.[2] An intensive program for teenagers, it was (and still is) a mashup of accelerated learning, personal development and physical challenge, the brainchild of the best thinkers and innovators in those worlds[3]. So two years before I could even drive, I spent 10 days completing Ropes Courses, learning brain science and being coached by Tony Robbins, Eric Jensen and an all-star cast of people in the business of changing lives.

In those 10 days, a light bulb came on in my head: "Maybe I'm not crazy. Maybe it's okay that I haven't bought into the whole system like everybody else has." I found out in those 10 days that I have a particular learning style that was definitely different from those my teachers were using, and we weren't connecting. I found out how to translate what I was being taught into my own style, relevance and Why, to get myself engaged. I got so into testing the tools I'd learned that they became the hook for me in classes. I went from being the nightmare student for my teachers to coming back from SuperCamp and proving another way—actually teaching workshops for them about how the brain works, how individual people learn differently, and how they could be teaching differently to make it more engaging and relevant to more kids.

I decided then that I was going to be an educator. Not because I was inspired by my own experience in school, but because I was committed to changing the system. I was committed to coming up with a way that people could learn, get the Why and have fun at the same time while stretching themselves. I believed that it didn't have a choice between working/learning intensely or having fun- that you could actually do both at once. I was committed to changing the system in that way.

The following summer I headed back to SuperCamp to be on staff, with the mission of learning how to create that "a-ha" experience for other people like I had myself. I spent the next 15 summers as a counselor, then trainer, then facilitator, then lead facilitator of those programs all over the world, apprenticing under—then ultimately working side by side with—the most brilliant minds in personal growth, alternative education and applied brain research in the world. I did what I do best—dug into the layers of why it worked, taking apart and putting back together the art of truly motivating people, creating transformative learning experiences, and leading people beyond what they thought was possible in their own capacity. I mastered how to set all of the conditions and interactions and content to create "a-ha" every time. I learned how to take groups of the best and brightest college students as staff and turn them into uber teams of leaders who could create deep process for teens, facilitate experiences, push themselves further than they knew possible and create energized magic for others every day for weeks at a time (on four to five hours of sleep per night).

Meanwhile I went off bright-eyed and excited to the number four college of education in the US to learn more. But by the end of my first year in the program, I almost got kicked out, mostly because I so vehemently disagreed with what I was being taught. Compared to what I was learning in real-life transformative teaching during the summers, the content in that program was antiquated and seemed from the dark ages. It didn't include any of the new brain research about how people actually learn (vs. how we've always been taught), which I was soaking up with the masters in my off-time. I found a few out-of-the-box professors I loved and learned from, fought with the rest, and stuck through it so I could get to the important part...teaching! After graduation, I moved to Chicago to teach high school on the south side, in an at-risk area where I found some forward-thinking superintendents looking for someone to try something new with a population most teachers avoided. I went there because I wanted to teach the kids who really didn't want to be at school. I got them. Plus my inner skeptic knew that if what I learned from those masters was really going to work in the world it had to work there, with these kids who had given up on school, surrounded by adults who had given up on them.

It was a pretty gang-infested area and kids had a really clear choice between coming to school or being on the street, where they could frankly make a lot of money and feel pretty significant in the world of drugs, turf, etc. I was teaching both ends of the spectrum: the kids who were way behind grade level, often truant and in trouble, and the highest of the high achievers. I had kids who were in ninth grade who read at a fourth- or fifth-grade level, rarely came to school and had all kinds of behavioral problems, and I had honors kids who were performing well in the system, engaging the way they'd learned from traditional school—listen, remember, apply, perform, repeat. I came in convinced I could change them all (get the disengaged to engage, the performers to rethink the way they were doing it to get to some real thinking and meaning) by doing it differently based on what I'd learned. I dove in, deciding to teach them all at the same level— actually, the honors level. But not like any of their other teachers had done it before.

Once I learned their language and earned their trust as being on their side, a great thing happened. I made contact. Kids got inspired. They got the Why. They started having fun while I pushed them in ways they hadn't experienced before. They started coming to school more often, and having success after success. In a relatively short time, my kids accelerated their learning, many jumping up a few levels after they left my class. I started getting attention for that. I started getting lots of observers in my classes, and inquiries about what I was doing. With an agenda to prove that a different way to teach could change everything, I documented what I was doing. I journaled. I started sharing what I was doing with other teachers.

While I was teaching, I started coursework toward my master's degree, as I co-wrote the book *Quantum Teaching: Orchestrating Student Success* with Mark Reardon and Bobbi Deporter, my mentors and cohorts at Supercamp, committed to making the art of unleashing genius and fun possible for teachers in classrooms. While colleges of education told us (much to our frustration about the very problem we were trying to solve) that QT wouldn't be accepted as a teachable text in their programs until it was printed and shelved for at least ten years, I'm proud to say that 14 years later QT is still a go-to manual for how to make content engaging, fun, tap all kinds of intelligences and learning styles while making learning an energized process that sticks.

Soon I realized that, while my favorite population is teenagers, I needed to teach teachers even more. For every teacher I could get to teach differently, how many kids could that impact? So I left my classroom to teach schools and auditoriums full of teachers. And many of them got it.

Shift in the way teachers and students experienced school started happening in entire systems, as teaching came alive and kids got sparked. Every summer, I kept building awesome teams of leaders to create impact in programs all over the globe. As I did both, I got feedback from people outside the world of education, that the very things I was teaching were needed in the business world, too.

So, I applied what I knew worked to spark insight and greatness for people, and built from there to bring impact to individuals and teams in the corporate world. I got phenomenal feedback that the tools I brought these leaders were taking people to a different level. All of a sudden, people who had been ready to quit were excited about their jobs. People who were coasting along started producing like crazy, getting results that they hadn't gotten before. And leaders started having more fun. They reported less stress, more impact, more results out of their people and built newly cohesive, strong teams.

Since then, I've consulted and coached in many industries, guiding leaders from retail store managers to Fortune 100 executives to bartenders to entrepreneurs to athletes to middle managers to select teams of disruptive ideates to college fraternity presidents to up-and-coming actors, giving them the tools that you're about to receive; the tools to take you from not just having people 'get it done,' but leading in an inspired way. People are going to remember you, and the effect you had on them far beyond wherever they thought they could be. I push pretty hard, insist on you asking yourself the tough questions, because I believe that the best answers are usually a few layers deep in your thinking. I will facilitate some peeling. I loved working with every leader I've every coached, because no two are alike, and I've been able to get to the heart and unlock the brilliant leader inside each one.

Now, you. Let's do this...